Rock Guitar

by Happy and Artie Traum

A Division of Music Sales Corporation,
33 West 60th Street, New York 10023

Library of Congress Card Catalogue Number 77-103823
International Standard Book Number 0-8256-2148-8

Cover and Book Design: Anne Abelman
Cover Photo: Miriam Bokser
Inside Photos: Linda Eastman
Elliot Landy
David Gahr
Raeburn Flerlage

Amsco Publishing Company
A Division of Music Sales Corporation
33 West 60th Street, New York 10023

Music Sales Limited
78 Newman Street, W1 London

Music Sales (Pty) Limited
27 Clarendon Street, Artarmon, Sydney, NSW, Australia

Printed in the United States

Table of Contents

Preface

My earliest musical memories have to do with sitting around a radio listening to Perry Como, Dean Martin and Doris Day sing the meaningless, commercial "pap" which seems to have characterized the early 1950's. A few years later disc jockeys were playing songs in a new style, then called a "passing fad", Rock n' Roll. Performers like Elvis Presley, Buddy Holly, Chuck Berry, Bill Haley, the Everly Brothers, the Crewcuts, and the Dell-Vikings (to name a few) cut a new image across the American musical scene; their music was driving, emotional and tight, and their personalities were eccentric and definable. These performers were immediately criticized by the adult world as being "wild", "unruly", "obscene", and "crude" and their music, well, "that wasn't music, it was just noise." All across the country, teen-agers were pressured against Rock n' Roll; I remember parents who forbade their kids to listen to it. "Oh, Elvis the Pelvis, he's just a hillbilly"; "It's all a lot of junk."; "How can they get away with those antics . . . it's downright obscene!" So it came to pass that Rock n' Roll was recognized, even if it was a negative recognition. The more the parents rejected the music, the more the kids loved it. Their reaction was not only rebellion against the older generation — the music was really exciting.

"Rock and Roll took the postwar blues singing style and set it against a slow rhythm of repetitive chords on the piano or guitar and an accentuated off-beat in the drums. The effect was overpowering."

Rock n' Roll had its roots in Negro "Rhythm and Blues" and Gospel music even though "Tin-Pan Alley" tried to water it down to a commercially palatable level. Samuel Charters, in his indispensable book *The Country Blues* describes Rock n' Roll as an outgrowth of the Blues:

Alan Freed, the disc jockey who coined the term "Rock n' Roll" in 1951, said that:

"Rock and Roll is really swing with a modern name. It began on the levees and plantations, took in folk songs, and features blues and rhythm."

Elvis Presley was strongly influenced by Negro blues singers from Mississippi, notably the singing of Big Boy Crudup, whose song *Rock Me, Mama* appears later in this book. Presley's early vocal styles are clearly derived from Blues stylization, and his songs (for ex. *Blue Suede Shoes, Heartbreak Hotel*) were mostly based upon the traditional 12-bar blues form (see Chapter III). Presley was, in fact, born in Tupelo, Mississippi, and he was a true "discovery." His first hit was a song called *That's All*

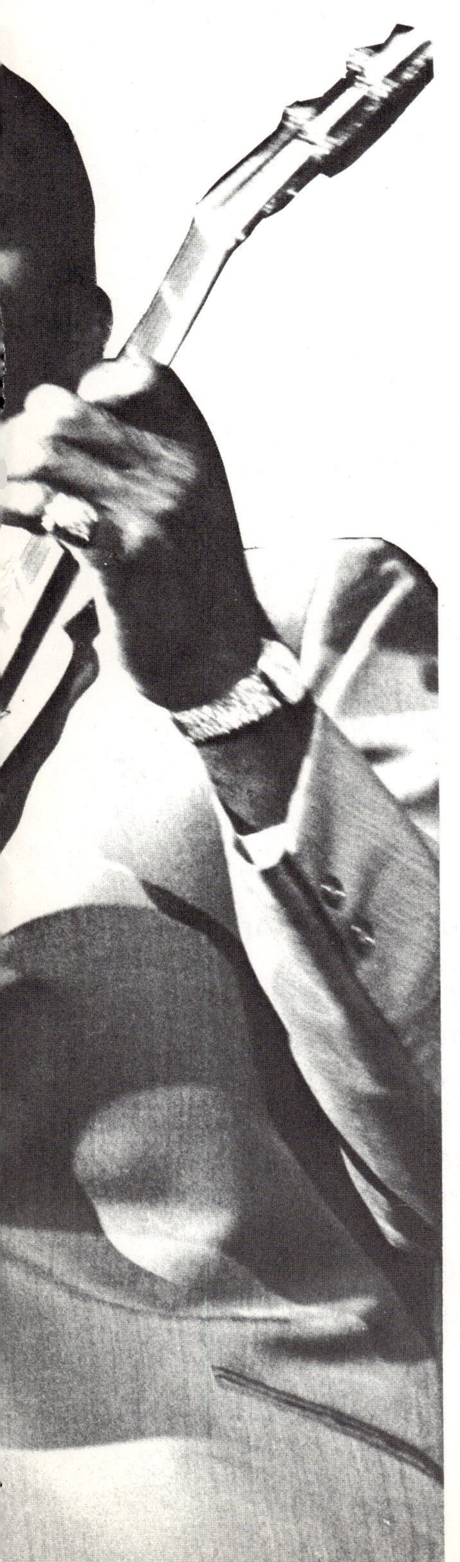

Right Mama and it sold hundreds of thousands of copies in the South. Soon afterwards Presley came to New York City, and Charters reports that he spent a good deal of time around the Apollo Theatre, listening to and studying Negro rhythm and Blues stars, especially Bo Diddely.

On the other hand, the music of The Everly Brothers was derived from white country music, "Bluegrass" and "Gospel," although they too were strongly influenced by the Blues. What captured the kids throughout America was the drive of the music, its intensity, and above all, its danceability. If you couldn't dance to it, it was worthless. So, the parents continued to criticize and the kids continued buying records. For better or for worse, Rock n' Roll was here to stay.

When I listen to early Rock n' Roll records I have very mixed feelings. Some of the songs are still great to listen to: *Get A Job, Dream, Hounddog.* The great majority were, I think, corrupted by imitation; after awhile they all began to sound alike, and worse, they became more and more wishy-washy, both musically and lyrically. By the time the late '50's had rolled around, Rock n' Roll was almost on the same low level as the "pap" which preceded it. Droves of young people, here and in England, turned to the purity and honesty of folk music. Folk music served a social function as well; it provided roots upon which young people could grow; it offered a sense of tradition and ritual in a world which seemed insane and chaotic. Folk music soon became equated with a youthful protest movement just as Rock n' Roll had been equated with juvenile delinquency a few years before.

It is unfortunate that parents (and sociologists) are quick to pin labels on anything they don't understand; thus, during the 50's there was a great deal of speculation as to whether a correlation could be drawn between juvenile delinquency and Rock n' Roll. I remember that the kids who joined gangs in New York always seemed to have a portable radio pressed against their ears; when they weren't terrorizing the schoolyard, they were harmonizing in three and four parts to new and standard tunes. Some of the best Rock n' Roll grew spontaneously out of the various local neighborhoods of our larger cities. Occasionally a lucky youngster was "discovered" and "made it to the top," enabling him to buy his proud parents a new car and a country home with a swimming pool (Rock n' Roll also functioned as part of the American Dream). But the important thing is that song writing was beginning to leave the hands of professional song writers. The folklorist Alan Lomax recognized in Rock n' Roll a new form of music and officially embraced it during his "Folksong '59" Concerts in Carnegie Hall. At this time, folk music had virtually replaced Rock n' Roll in its mass appeal.

Reading the New York Times during the period 1955-1959 shows incident after incident related to Rock n' Roll. Rock n' Roll "shows" and movies created storms wherever they appeared. The movie *Rock Around The Clock* caused or rather, led to "riots" in scores of cities all around the world and ultimately led to the banning of Rock n' Roll in St. Louis, Egypt and Iraq. One of the major disturbances occurred in 1957 when Alan Freed presented a Rock n' Roll show at the Paramount Theatre in New York. The next day the headlines read:

"ROCK AND ROLL TEENAGERS TIE UP TIMES SQUARE AREA" and "TEENS RIOT IN TIMES SQUARE"

The story in the New York Times said:

"... the rock and rollers stamped their feet so vigorously in the theatre that firemen became alarmed . . . the management cleared ¾ of the 1600 youngsters from the balcony as a precautionary measure ..."

Alan Freed countered reports of violence with comments like this one,

"These are not bad kids, they are just enthusiastic ..."

The kids themselves had relatively simple answers for their attraction to the music; one 15-year-old girl told a New York Times reporter:

"It's just instinct, that's all. I come to hear it because I can sing and scream ..."

Psychiatrists, social workers, priests, parents, educators, journalists, all feeling threatened by Rock n' Roll's influence on the younger generation, formulated complex theories about the "social function" of Rock n' Roll and the moral issues involved. A relatively moderate psychiatric social worker put it this way:

"Kids, just like adults, get caught in a mass kind of hysteria which is contagious . . . this behavior is part of their individual as well as collective or group rebellion against the strictness of adult society."

(Dr. A. D. Buchmueller/N. Y. Times Jan. 12, 1958)

Other psychiatrists drew parallels between Rock n' Roll and

rhythmic behavior patterns of the Middle Ages. Dr. Joost A. M. Meerlo at Columbia University likened the Rock n' Roll frenzy to *St. Vitus' Dance,* the "contagious epidemic of dance fury" which swept the Middle Ages. He went on:

"The Children's Crusade and the Tale of The Pied Piper remind us of these seductive, contagious dance furies . . ."

Young people were dancing

"more and more into a prehistoric rhythmic trance until they had gone far beyond all the accepted versions of human dancing (sic)

and

"Rock and roll is a sign of depersonalization of the individual, of ecstatic veneration of mental decline and passivity. If we cannot stem the tide with its waves of rhythmic narcosis and of future waves of vicarious craze, we are preparing our own downfall in the midst of pandemic funeral dances."

This is quite a mouthful, even for a college professor, and it helped to distort the nature of Rock n' Roll for the academic and intellectual community. What does he mean by "accepted versions of human dancing"; is the *Minuet* the only polite means of bodily expression? Rock n' Roll was beginning to challenge the stuffy, cold, inflexible attitudes of American and Continental society. It is no wonder then that Southern racists called Rock n' Roll an "integrationist, Communist plot"; they were alarmed by the fusion of white and Negro music and dance.

Shortsightedness about Rock n' Roll was not a monopoly of Southern racists and stuffy moralists. A world-wide phenomenon, Rock n' Roll soon entered the political arena. While Americans called Rock n' Roll a "Communist plot", the Russians called it "disgusting music" which was indicative of "Western decadence." The Communists were so alarmed by the music that delegates from eight countries (Nov. 1, 1958) called for better jazz from Eastern Europe to "combat Rock and Roll." Egyptian officials banned the music in 1957 as "imperialist trash" but the New York Times reported that:

"rock and roll still has a fascination among the sons and daughters of Egypt's elite."

The issue is far from dying. The Cuban government officially scorns Rock n' Roll while the South Vietnamese government went so far as to ban it from the radio on April 1, 1963.

Saigon, April 1—
"The South Vietnamese government, which in the past banned all dancing and singing of sad songs, banned even the singing of twist songs today . . . the reason given for the banning of the twist was that it was not compatible with the country's morality law and its anti-Communist struggle." (sic)

Well, is it a Communist plot or a Capitalist plot? Is it an Integrationist plot or an anti-religious plot? Pope Paul himself felt compelled to comment on Rock n' Roll in July of 1965 when he warned some ten thousand schoolgirls against *"frenzied agitation over some foolish entertainers."*

A year later John Lennon of the Beatles was branded an "anti-Christ" and a campaign was begun in the South and Midwest to discredit his phenomenal reputation.

It should be apparent to everyone that Rock n' Roll was neither a Communist plot nor a Capitalist plot nor a plot of the devil to "rule the hearts of men". Let it be said that in its relatively short existence (15 years in musical development is virtually nothing) Rock n' Roll has represented a musical and psychological break between the generations. The younger generation has simply created its own set of symbols, its own ritualization to cope with an insane adult world. While politicians hacked it out on the floors of Senates, and while mercenaries and revolutionaries fought it out on the battlefields of the world, the kids were searching for something to relate to and attach themselves to. While reading through newspaper reports I was amused to find that while psychologists were having a field day with teen-age behavior, tanks were rumbling through the streets of Budapest and Havana, jets strafed villages in Vietnam, and Kennedy and Khrushchev played nuclear games of chicken over the telephone.

Folk music temporarily replaced Rock n' Roll because it dealt directly with true-life situations and incidents; it was doomed to fade out because it expressed the reality of a time which had already passed. A new music was needed to express *now,* with all of the beauty and chaos we associate with the present. Basically alienated from mainstream America, young people found personal expression in the songs of the Beatles and Bob Dylan, the two giants of the *new* music. Their music was straight and honest; it was personal and it refused to hide reality under a pile of glittering clichés which told of a make-believe world; this music told young people about themselves and about the reality of their everyday lives. Dylan once said of his songs:

"I carry a song in my head for a long time and then it comes bursting out . . ."

BOB DYLAN

JOHN SEBASTIAN

The implication is that he alone has total control over the song; it is not controlled by the demands of the market. Dylan's story is a retelling of musical changes in the American scene: brought up on "pop" music, he abandoned it for "folk" and "country" music, listening to and emulating such great singers and instrumentalists as Hank Williams, Leadbelly, Mance Lipscomb and above all Woody Guthrie. Soon he began writing songs in the folk idiom, but he was dissatisfied with imitation. His style is continually changing and developing. There is no doubt that Dylan and the Beatles influenced each other, but they were all highly influenced by the great artists who preceded them (see Tree). The Lennon-McCartney tune *I'm A Loser* is written in the unmistakable Dylan style, but one can hear traces of Woody Guthrie and Leadbelly in the song.

In the wake of the "Folk Revival" hundreds of young people began writing their own songs; most of them have never been heard of, but some have made it to the top. John Sebastian, of the Lovin' Spoonful, has written several hit tunes, and most of these (for example, *Daydream*) are written like the old ragtime-jugband tunes. John himself had his first group experience in 1963 with a local aggregation called "The Even Dozen Jug Band", all twelve of whom had a devoted interest in recreating the Jug Band sound of the 1920's. They listened to and admired groups like The Cannon Jug Stompers and one can hear traces of Gus Cannon in the "good-time sound" of the Spoonful. It is interesting to note that all of the members of the "Even Dozen" found themselves placed highly in the musical scene: one plays lead guitar for the Fugs, one is in The Blues Project, one produces records, one composed the well-known "Baroque Beatles" recording. I think that there has been a concerted attempt of all of these young musicians to exchange musical and social ideas. Thus, recent jam sessions in New York have shown B. B. King, Buddy Guy, Jimi Hendrix, Paul Butterfield and others to be acutely aware of an identity based upon musical and social ideals.

B. B. KING

BUDDY GUY

JIMI HENDRIX

The guitar found its place in Rock n' Roll through Negro "Rhythm and Blues" groups which worked out of Chicago in the late '40s and early '50s and which still exist today. Most of the great R & B artists never reached national popularity until recently when their songs were "revived" by groups like The Rolling Stones, The Moody Blues, The Animals and more recently The Blues Project and The Paul Butterfield Blues Band.

I had never heard of most of the great R & B groups until just a few years ago, but now names like Muddy Waters, Howlin' Wolf, Elmo' James, Little Walter, Jimmy Reed (the list goes on and on) are part of my everyday vocabulary. There is no question but that a significant change in guitar stylization developed from these early R & B groups. Elmo James, Howlin' Wolf, Muddy Waters etc., all began playing in Mississippi and were all influenced by the singing and guitar styles of the great Charlie Patton and Robert Johnson (see Discography). All of these men know each other and all exchanged ideas as they moved from Mississippi to Chicago and started their own bands. Elmo James, whose famous song *Dust My Broom* has inspired many guitarists, sings in the deep, gutsy Mississippi tradition, as do Wolf and Waters. The great songs which I remember for their guitar parts are too numerous to be listed here, but it is hard to forget Muddy Waters' sliding guitar on *Going Down To Louisiana,* or the figure for *Hoochie-Coochie Man* or Howlin' Wolf's *Smokestack Lightnin',* or B. B. King's *Slow and Easy Blues.*

B. B. King, Freddy King, and Albert King, who all bear the same last name but who are not related other than in musical stylization, all helped to develop electric blues guitar. The most famous King, B. B., worked as a plantation worker and stevedore in Mississippi, but he had been playing guitar since the age of 6, and was destined to become a disc jockey and eventually a performer of national renown. B. B. King's guitar style is based upon the traditional 12-bar blues form but his rhythmic ideas are so unique that he seems to fade in and out of the structure. His melody lines weave back and forth, he throws in a surprising high note suddenly, stretches it until the tension is almost unbearable, then stops for a second of silence, and finally brings the phrase to a conclusion. The effect is intensely exciting.*

*For more on B. B. King, see the interview by Stanley Dance, the transcriptions from his playing, starting on page 102.

MUDDY WATERS

Chuck Berry is another great guitar player who is beyond classification. I am continually amazed by the spontaneity of his solo work, and by the light feeling he gets in his playing. If anyone can be called the "Father" of rock guitar playing, Chuck Berry is the man.

Of course, there are scores of great guitarists. One blues-oriented guitarist with more sophisticated musical ideas is Curtis Mayfield, the brilliant arranger and guitarist for the Impressions. His lines are very simple but always to the point; not a single note is extraneous. Listen to his playing on *People Get Ready* and *The Woman's Got Soul.* It is a delight.

CHUCK BERRY

JIMI HENDRIX

There are many younger musicians who are inspired by these and other great R & B guitarists, and are trying to grow with and develop on the musical heritage of the blues. These men are aware of how much they can learn from the older guitarists, and are listening carefully to them. But they add to their playing the feeling and experience drawn from their own lives, which makes their music meaningful and relevant to the present. Robbie Robertson (The Band), Eric Clapton (The Cream), Mike Bloomfield (The Electric Flag), and Jimi Hendrix, are some of those important lead guitarists. We have included a Discography in the appendix of this book to set a direction for your listening.

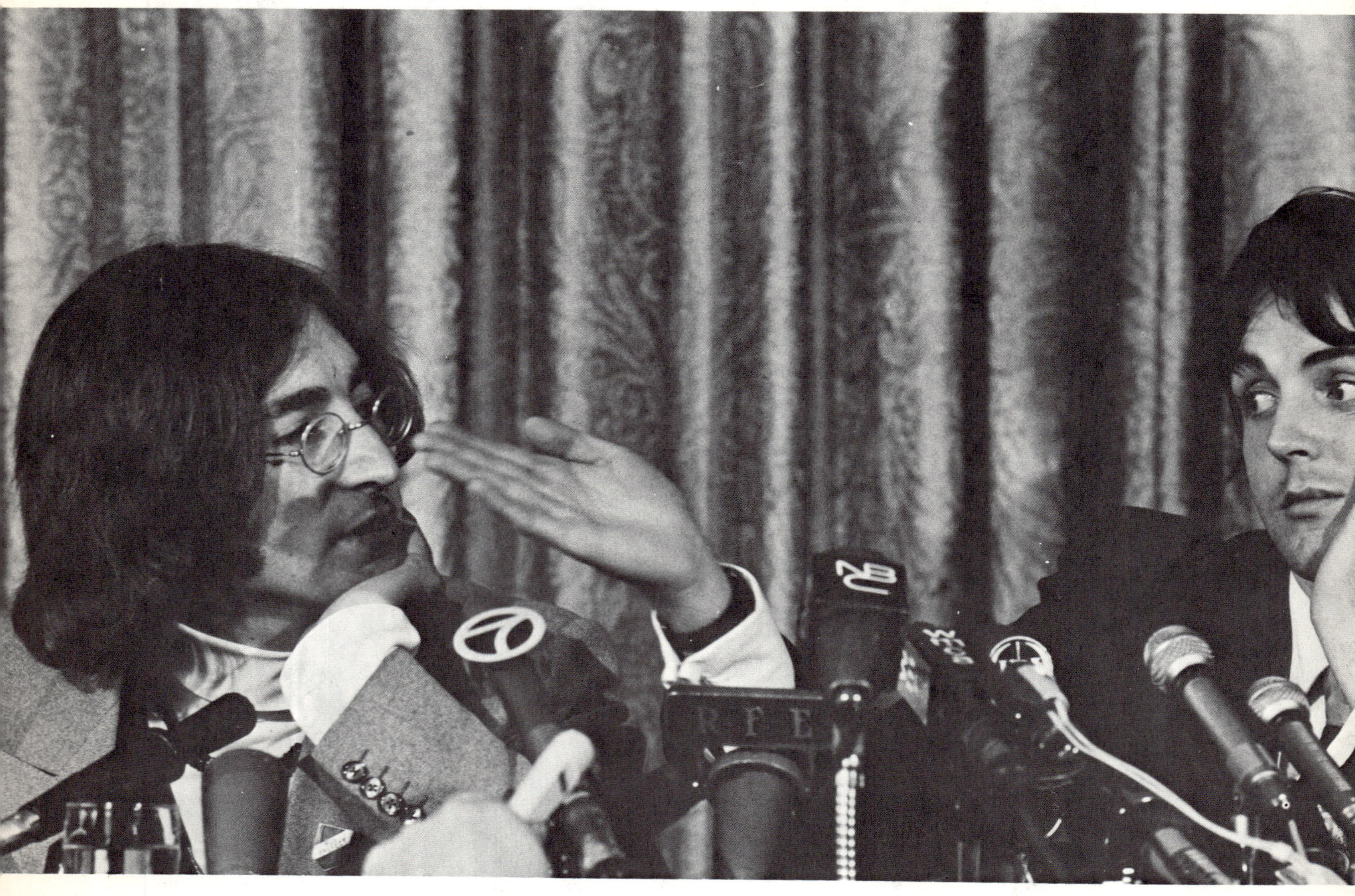

JOHN LENON AND PAUL McCARTNEY

Introduction

This book was written for those who like and want to play Rock n' Roll Guitar. It is a guide, a leader, for the student who knows some guitar, but just can't seem to get ahead on his own. It is meant to be used by someone who wants to make music that is exciting, powerful and bluesy, in as simple or complex a way as he wishes. Like folk music, Rock n' Roll can be played with a limited amount of musical training, but can also be the object of years of intensive study. We have designed this book so the student can begin playing immediately, getting the background in rhythm guitar that is so necessary to one's becoming a good lead guitarist. We have avoided scales and exercises, as much as possible, putting in their place simple riffs and chords that can be used both as exercises and as working examples of good Rock guitar.

A glance through the pages will show you that this is not a book for absolute beginners. The student should have a working knowledge of the basic chords and strums usually associated with song accompaniment before attempting to use this book. If you do not already know them, the following chords should be studied and practiced until they can be played easily:

These diagrams are standard guitar chord frames. The top line of each diagram represents the nut of the guitar; the first line below it is the first fret on the neck, and so on. The dots and numbers represent the placement of the fingers on the strings: Bass E on the left, treble E on the right. Index finger is 1, middle finger is 2, ring finger is 3, pinky is 4. An X above the line representing a string means that string should not be played.

Chord Chart

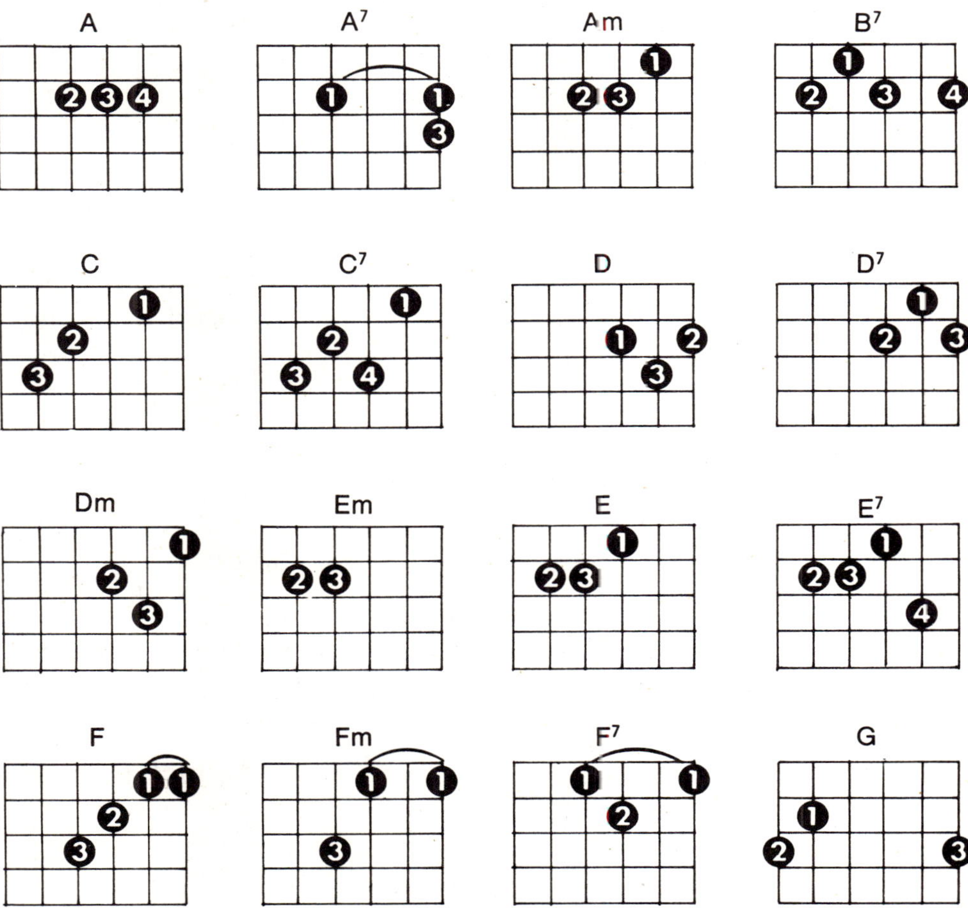

In addition to the standard guitar notation, many guitar parts are written in a guitar Tablature as a substitute for, or a supplement to, the music. The tablature can be extremely useful for those who do not yet read music, or for those who read but want to see the exact positions on the guitar that the notes are played.

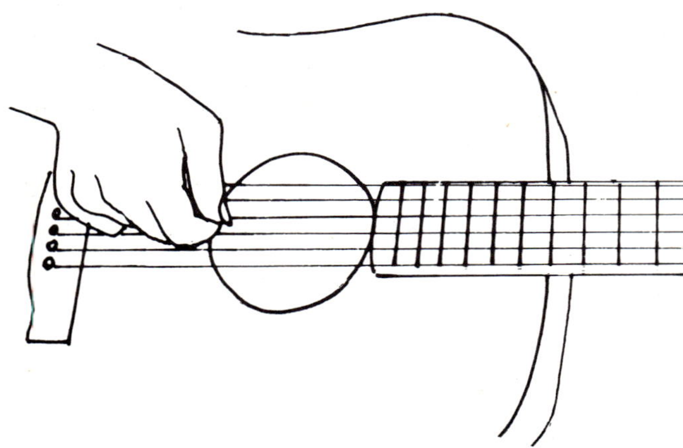

The guitar tabulature has six lines; each one representing a string on the guitar. The lowest line is the 6th string (or bass E) and the highest is the 1st (or treble E):

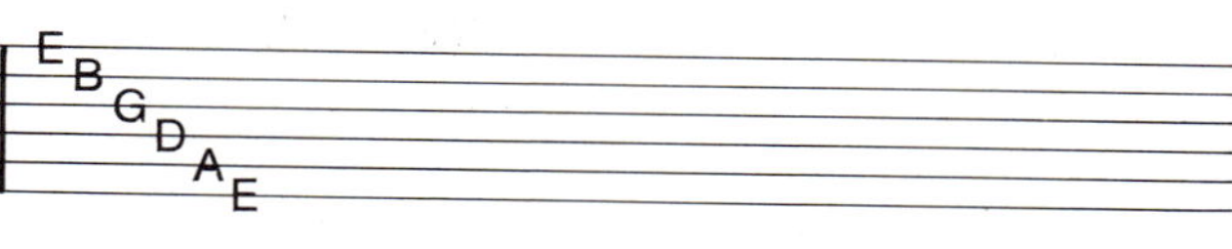

A number on one of the lines shows the fret at which that string is depressed (fretted). Therefore:

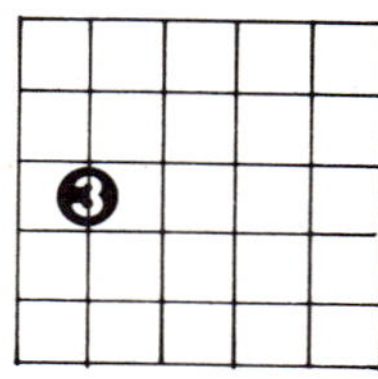

means that the 5th string is depressed on the third fret giving the note C. An entire C chord would look like this:

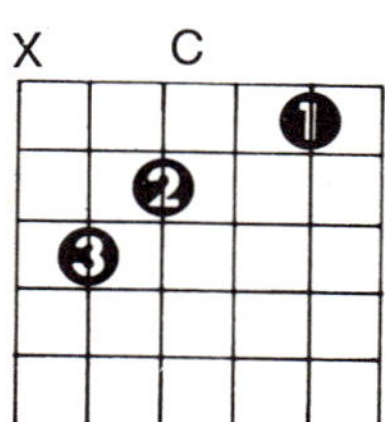

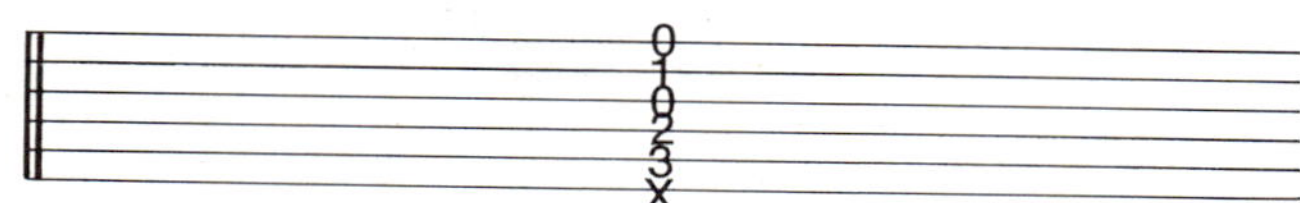

As you can see, the principle is easy and practical no matter where on the fingerboard you might want to play. A high E would look like this:

and a high E chord is written in this manner:

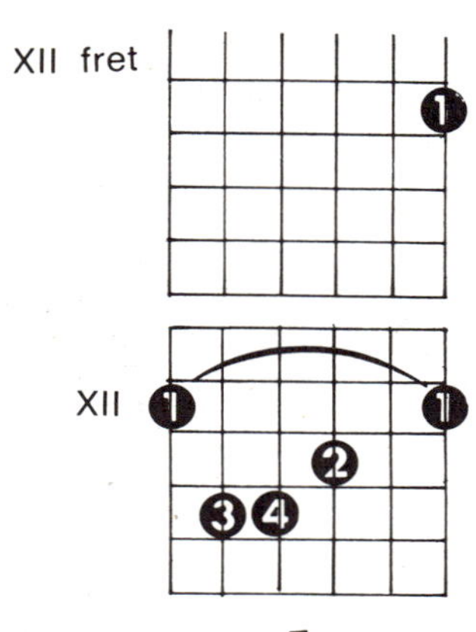

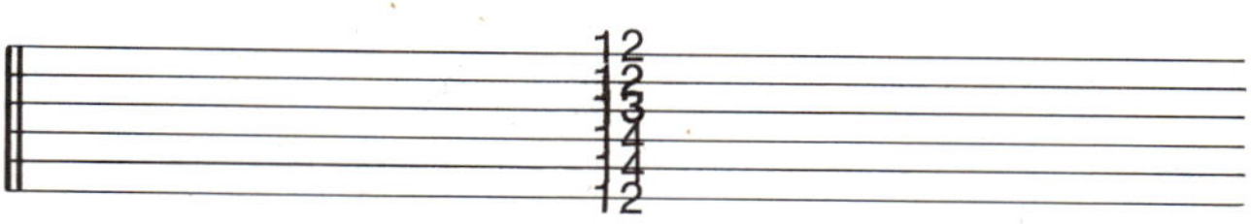

Various symbols can be used to show accents; for example ∾ represents a *slur* (stretching a string at a given fret, thereby raising the pitch). **H** stands for "hammering on" or plucking a string and changing its pitch before the string stops ringing. ↓ represents a stroke down over the strings with the pick, while ↑ is an upstroke. Here's an example:

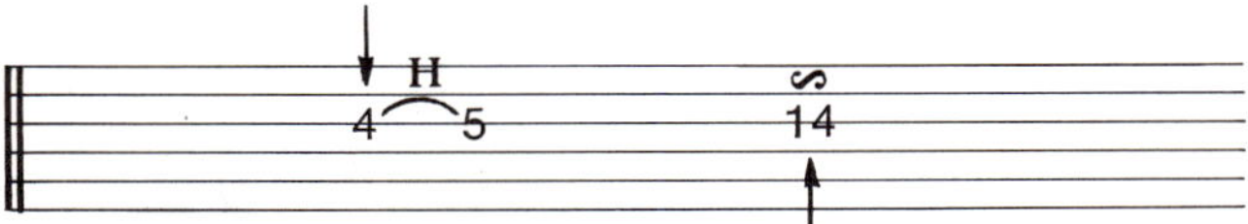

The following notation shows a common lead guitar run.

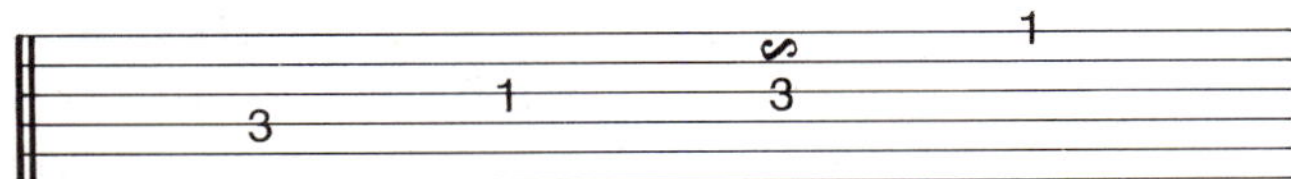

In addition you might want to notate the specific tone of both the guitar and the amplifier. Full treble is written FT and full bass is FB. This is especially important for the rhythm guitarist whose part is often written as block chords:

Sometimes the rhythm guitarist plays only part of a chord, in a particular inversion, and with a specific setting. This can be fully notated, as follows:

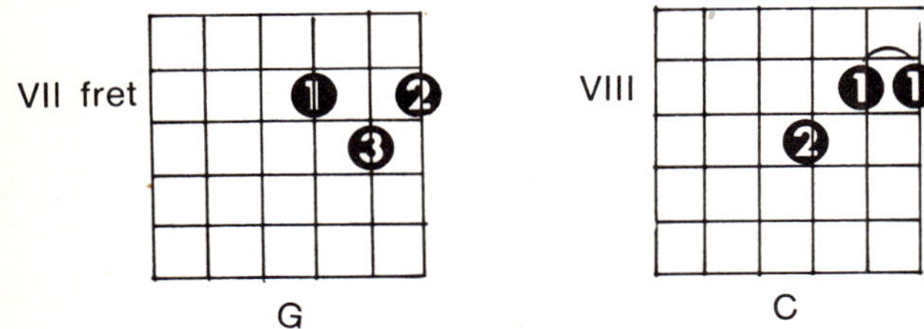

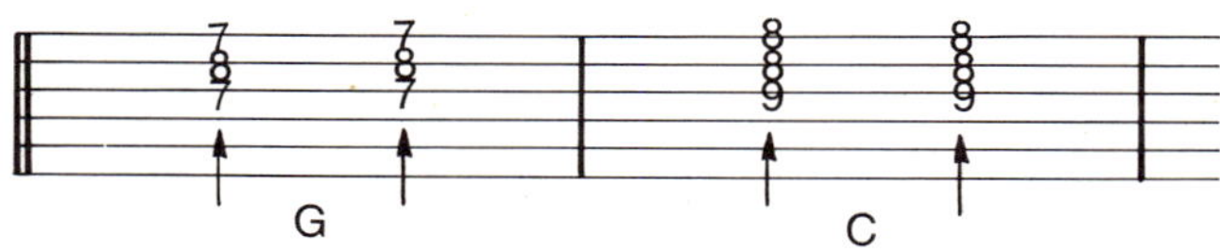

The most important prerequisite for using this book is a love of, and an ear for, the rock idiom. A musician cannot take music from a printed page and make it swing without knowing what swinging music sounds like. (Have you ever heard an opera singer trying to sing blues while reading from sheet music?) Therefore, it is essential to listen to as many rock guitarists as possible, on recordings, or preferably, in person. Throughout this book we make references to guitarists whom we admire for their taste and creativity. Evaluate lead guitar breaks and rhythm guitar patterns. This is the way ot learn — by developing your ear along with your fingers.

In preparing a book of instruction in an area as diffuse and changing as Rock n' Roll, many obvious problems arise; mainly, what to put in and what to leave out. We have chosen to emphasize the Rhythm and Blues aspects of Rock guitar playing, partially because it is our favorite sound, and partially because it is in this area that the guitar is the dominant instrument. But, we have included a cross-section of other styles to give the student as solid a background in Rock guitar as possible. We feel that we have been successful in providing a vehicle by which a student can become a good Rock guitarist, and in documenting what has become a national (and international) music of enormous popularity.

We will show the music, but what we cannot show, of course, is how to be creative with what we have provided. That part is up to you. You must digest the material, play with it, adapt it, listen to it, and eventually come up with something that is your own — something that represents you.

Happy and Artie Traum

Rhythm Guitar

Rhythm is the most important part of Rock n' Roll guitar playing; after all, it is the foundation upon which the entire musical structure depends. Although the drummer and bass players are responsible for keeping the beat strong and steady, the rhythm guitarist must provide the background chords around which the singer, lead guitarist and harp player can work. Rhythm guitar can make or break a song. Groups with poor rhythm guitarists seem to fall apart. They lack strength and drive.

Generally, the rhythm guitarist plays what sounds like a very simple part over and over again. But don't be deceived by this simplicity: it is not easy to play rhythm guitar correctly. I have seen scores of guitarists banging away at the strings as though they were making an overhand smash on the tennis court. Unfortunately, they just don't make it. The rhythm guitarist must be especially sensitive to the other members of the group and he must be careful not to clutter the overall sound. Even after you have mastered the rhythms in this section, it may take years before you are really comfortable with them, and before you can develop your own style.

We have begun this section with a study of barre chords, followed by the use of these chords in various rhythmic exercises. Soon, you will be playing songs like *Earth Angel* and *The Midnight Hour* in much the same way they are played on the original recordings. When you play these rhythms it is essential that you get a clear, crisp sound. Every string which you cover must be pressed down tightly, and those which should be dampened must not be heard at all. If you play correctly you will find your wrist and forearm getting quite sore at first; rhythm guitar playing is hard work!

Certain well-known songs provide excellent examples of solid rhythm guitar patterns. Listen, for example to:

"Fanny Mae"/Buster Brown, "Meet Me At the Bottom"/Howlin' Wolf, "She's a Woman"/Beatles, "Yesterday"/Beatles, "I'm Lookin' Thru You"/Beatles, "High-Heeled Sneakers"/Tommy Tucker, "Daydream"/Spoonful, "Let the Little Boy Rock and Roll"/Spoonful, "Dust My Broom"/Elmo James, and "Runnin' & Hidin' "/Jimmy Reed.

twelve bar blues

As we have said, Negro music of the rural South, especially Mississippi and Alabama, has been the major influence on contemporary American popular music. Therefore, it is essential that anyone learning to play Rock should be thoroughly familiar with the blues, and especially twelve-bar blues, the dominant blues form. Thousands of songs have been written in a twelve-bar progression, making up a good percentage of our country blues, rhythm and blues, and rock n' roll songs, including many of the biggest popular hits. It is a progression that every jazz and pop musician knows, and it will be the basis for many of the songs and examples in this book.

The following pattern should be played over and over again, until it becomes second nature, and you can feel the changes without even thinking about them. We'll start in the key of E:

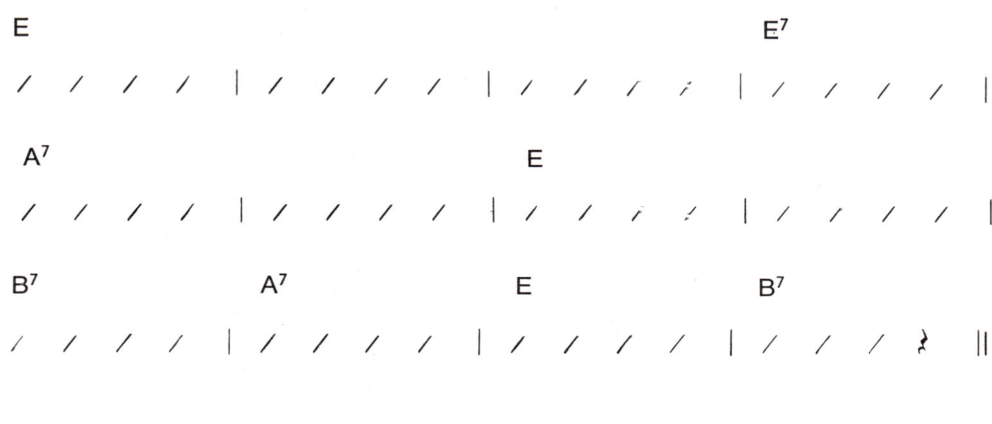

Here is the same progression in A:

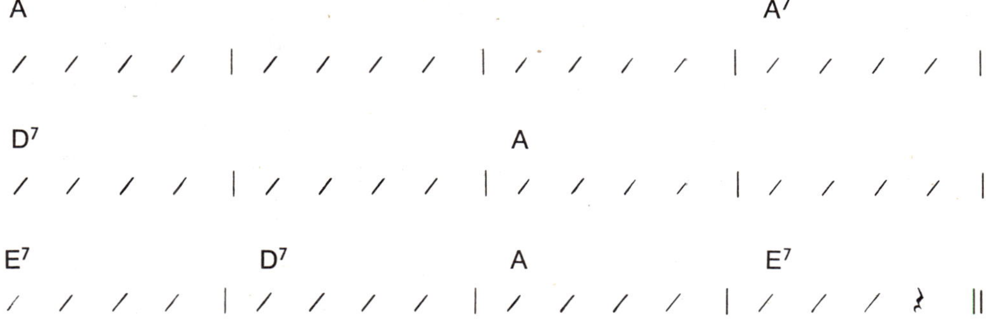

The lyrics of the 12-bar blues usually fit into a pattern also. They are often three-line stanzas, in which the first line repeats, followed by a rhyming line. For example:

My baby left me, she even took my shoes,
I said, my baby left me, even took my shoes.
She didn't leave me nothin' but them awful lowdown blues.

In another type of 12-bar blues lyric, the first two lines rhyme, followed by a chorus that repeats after each verse:

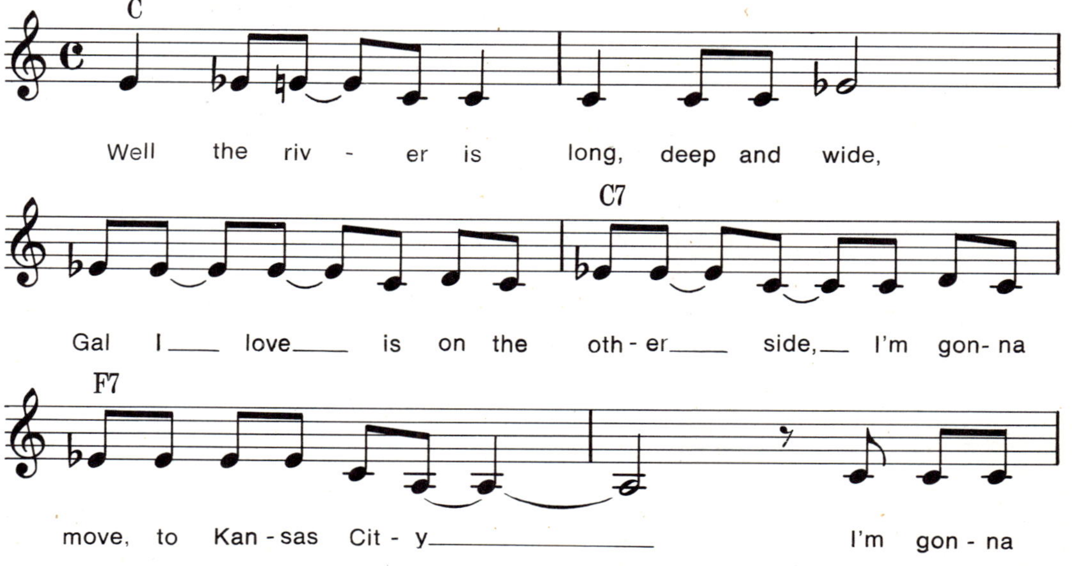

Here is a well-known 12-bar blues that has recently been made into a rock n' roll hit:

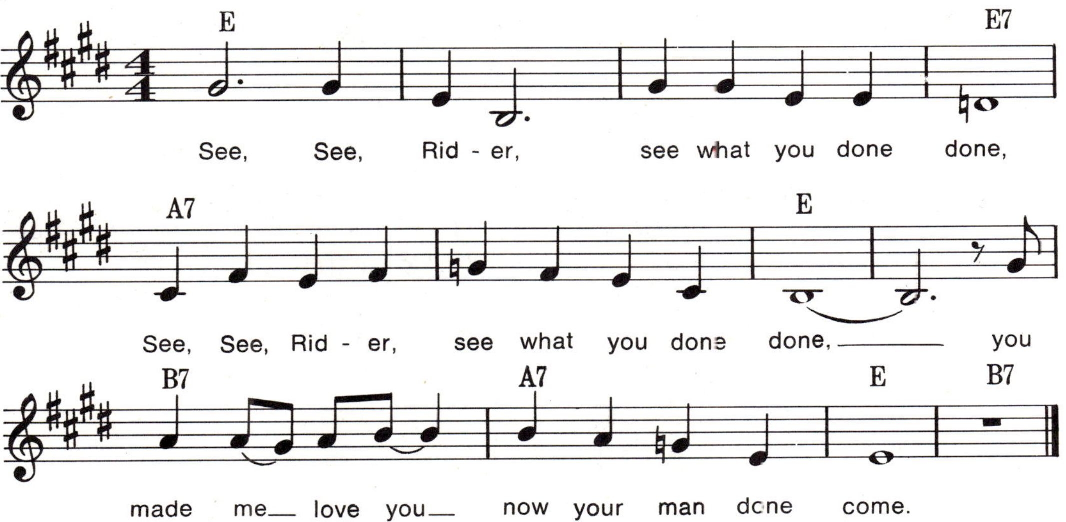

Once you are familiar with the twelve-bar blues progression, you will notice that after each singing line there is a pause of several beats, in which nothing seems to be happening:

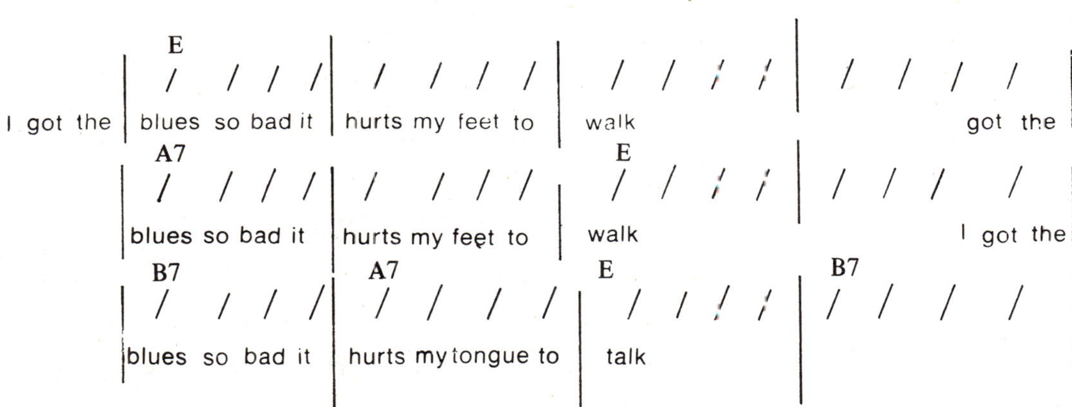

These holes in the singing are natural places of the guitar to fill in with blues runs. It seems as though they are left there especially for this purpose, to allow the instrument a chance to "answer" the singer, creating a dialogue between the voice and the guitar. A good blues guitarist should be able to improvise these *runs* (also called riffs, fills, breaks) and the most admired musician is the one who can make the most tasteful and original *runs.* (There will be specific information on how to create these runs in the Lead Guitar section of this book.)

Reference: Country blues singers, Charlie Patton, Robert Johnson, Skip James, Big Bill Broonzy, Lightnin' Hopkins. Chicago blues singers Jimmy Reed, Howlin' Wolf, Muddy Waters, B. B. King, Otis Rush, Junior Wells. Contemporary Rock n' Roll artists who rely upon the blues form; Chuck Berry, The Rolling Stones, The Moody Blues, Jimi Hendrix, The Cream.

barre chords

Barre chords are essential to the rhythm guitarist. These are made by fretting all six strings with the first finger, and then making a chord above that barre. Thus, if you barre the fifth fret and play an E chord above the barre, you get a full A chord. It looks like this:

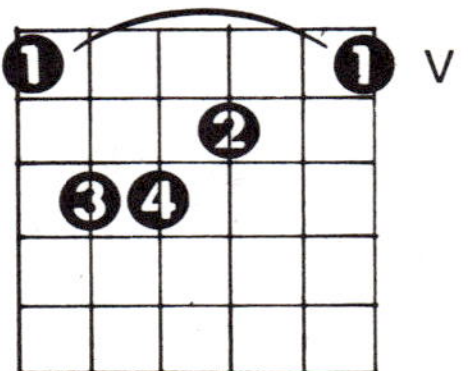

Making a chord in this way is similar to using a capo. As you move the barre up the neck of the guitar, the chord is raised by a half-step at each fret. If you barre the first fret and place your fingers in the E chord position, you will have an F chord (the E chord raised one fret). Barring the second fret gives you an F♯, the third fret a G, and so on.

The complete set is: E F F♯ G G♯ A A♯ B C C♯ D D♯ E

Notice that there is no E♯ or B♯. The scale can also be seen in terms of flats:

E F G♭ G A♭ A B♭ B C D♭ D E♭ E

There is no F♭ or C♭.

Try the following chords with the E position barre, strumming down across all of the strings with your pick.

G (E pos III) A (E pos V) B (E pos VII) C (E pos VIII)

Now try to find these chords with the barred E position.

C♯; F♯; D; A♭; E♭; B♭.

The same chord positions can be made into minor chords by using the Em formation above the barre. Thus, if you barre the first fret the chord would be Fm, and it would look like this:

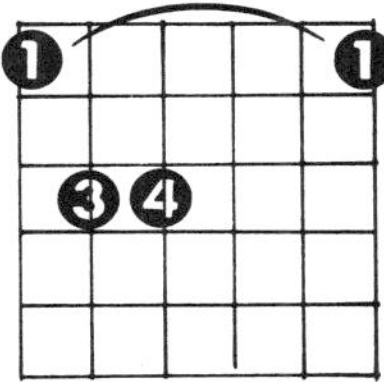

Similarly, for an F♯m, barre the second fret; for a Gm barre the third fret, and so on. Using this method, find the following chords:

G♯m; B♭m; Cm; Dm; Bm.

Barre chords can also be made using the A and Am positions. If you barre the first fret and make an A position above it, you will have an A♯ (or B♭) chord.

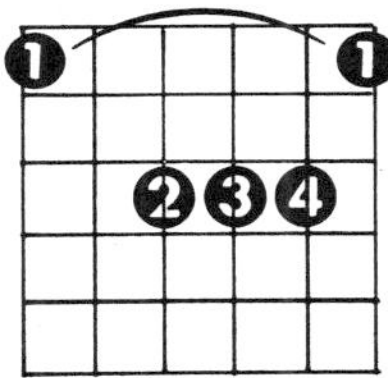

The same chord formation at the third fret would be C, while at the fifth fret the chord would be D, etc. The same sequence would be true using the Am position:

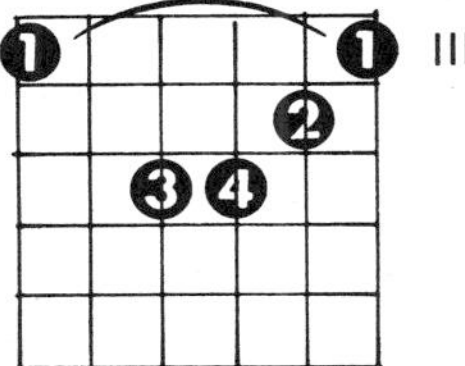

Find the following chords using the barred A or Am positions.

Bm; C♯; Dm; E♭; F♯m.

By now you should have a fairly good idea of how to make barre chords, and how to find the ones you want. To play solid, effective rhythm, you should be able to grab any chord you like in at least two, and preferably, three positions. For example, C can be played in its first position, by barring the third fret and making an A formation, and by barring the eighth fret and making an E formation.

Try the following progressions, used in many songs, as exercises. Each diagonal line represents a stroke across all of the strings with the pick.

Seventh chords, essential to blues, can also be formed with barre positions. The E7 and A7 formations are the most widely used. They look like this:

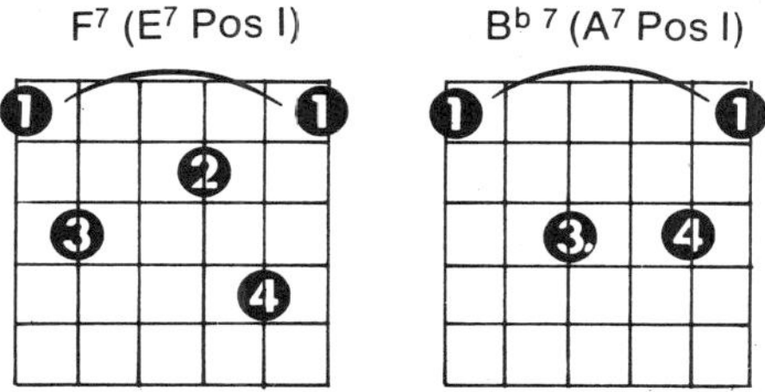

Before going on, familiarize yourself with these chord positions.

Using both the E7 and A7 formations, find the following chords:

F♯7; C7; E♭7; B7.

Although these barred seventh chords are used a great deal, other movable seventh chords are very useful too. The C7 position looks like this:

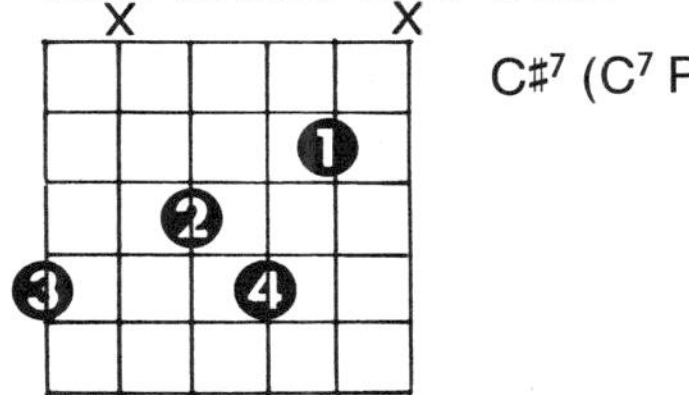

It is important to notice the x marks over the first and fifth strings in the diagram. This means that these strings should not be heard; they are *damped* with the left hand, which touches those strings and stops them from vibrating.

Another movable chord position which is very useful is the B7:

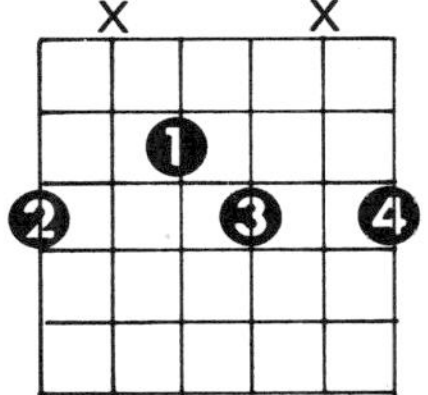

Now try the following chords as substitute possibilities for the traditional 12-bar blues form:

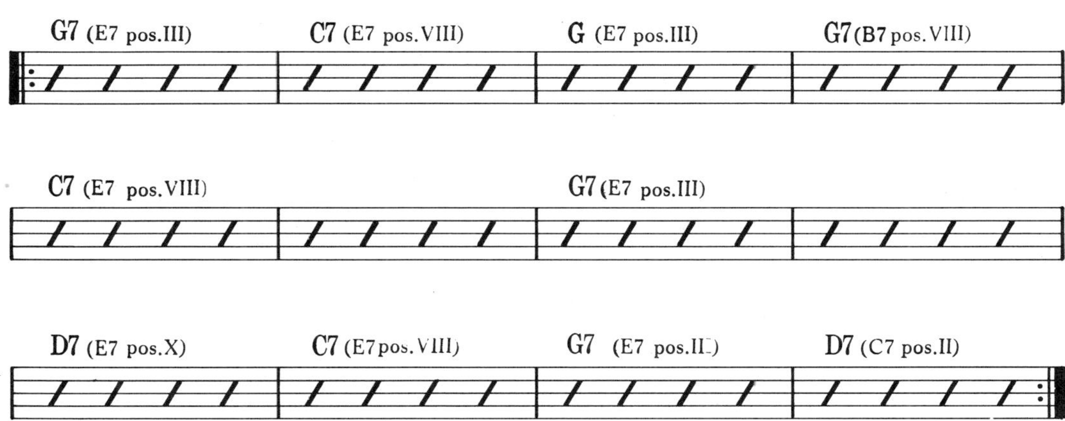

As you can see, you have a great variety in your choice of positions. The same progression could be played like this:

G7 (C7 pos. VIII) | C7 | G7 (C7 pos. VIII) |

|: / / / / | / / / / | / / / / | / / / / |

C7 (A7 pos.III) | C7 (E7 pos.VIII) | G7 (C7 pos. VIII) |

| / / / / | / / / / | / / / / | / / / / |

D7 (A7 pos V) | C7 (A7 pos. III) | G7 (E7 pos. III) | D7 (E7 pos. X)

| / / / / | / / / / | / / / / | / / / / :|

Here are some rhythm chords in the key of E:

E (A pos. VII) | A7 (E7 pos. V) | E (A pos. VII) | E7 (B7 pos. VI)

/ / / / | / / / / | / / / / | / / / / |

A7 (E7 pos. V) | | E (A pos. VII) |

/ / / / | / / / / | / / / / | / / / / |

B7 (E7 pos. VII) | A7 (E7 pos. V) | E (A pos. VII) A7 (E7 pos. V) | E C7 B7

/ / / / | / / / / | / / / / | / / / 𝄽 ||

A slightly more complicated chord structure within a blues framework might go like this:*

E | G♯7 (E7 pos. IV) | E7 (B7 pos. VI) | A7 (E7 pos. V)

/ / / / | / / / / | / / / / | / / / / |

E C#7 (C7 pos. II) | F7 (C7 pos. VII) B7 (E7 pos. VII) | B7 (E7 pos. VII) | E E7 A Am

/ / / / | / / / / | / / / / | / / / / |

E C7 B7

/ / / / ||

Here is the same progression in A:*

A (E pos. V) | C♯7 (C7 pos. II) | A7 (E7 pos. V) | D7 (C7 pos. III)

/ / / / | / / / / | / / / / | / / / / |

*Several songs can be sung to this progression, including *Trouble in Mind* and *Georgia On My Mind.*

E7 (B7 pos. VI)
A (E pos. V) F♯7 (C7 pos. VII) B7 (E7 pos. VII) A A7 D Dm A

/ / / / | / / / / | / / / / | / / / 𝄽 ||

In the early days of Rock n' Roll, there was one chord progression that was used so often that it became a cliche, almost synonymous with the term "Rock n' Roll":

C, Am, Dm, G7

Hundreds of tunes were written around this chord pattern, including hits like *Earth Angel, Dream, Sh-Boom,* and *Silhouettes.* I'm sure you recognize this progression. Try playing it with these barre chords: (The rhythm given here is in *triplets,* that is, three down strums to one beat. Count *one,* two, three, *one,* two, three.)

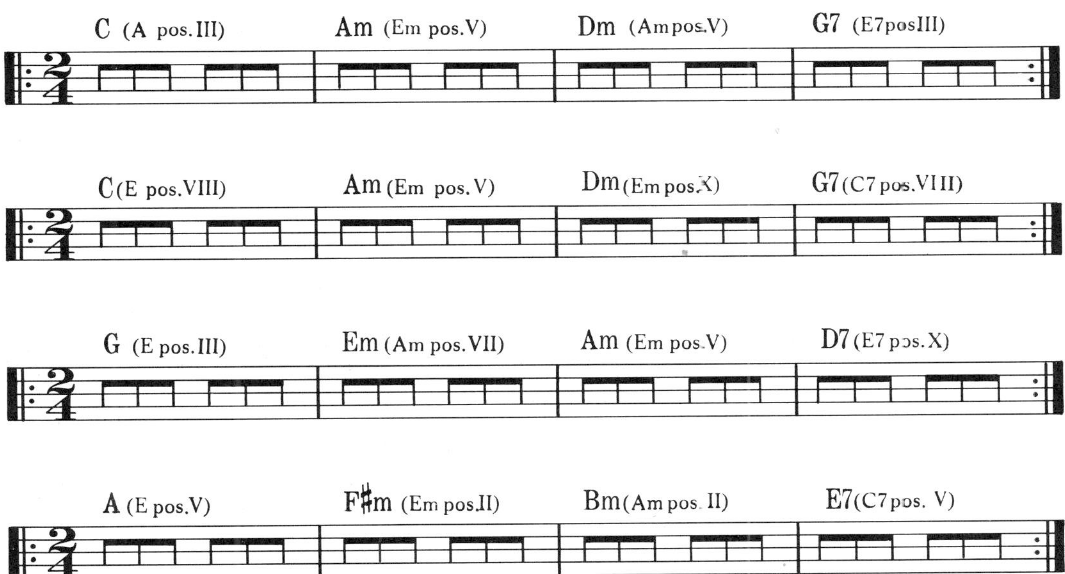

Respect

This song, Respect, by Otis Redding Jr., became a smash hit when Aretha Franklin recorded it for Atlantic Records. It is an ideal song to practice barre chords with, and will build up your wrist muscles as you practice. We have put the rhythmic accent on the two and the four beats of each measure; thus, you should count: one, two, *three,* four.

F (E pos. I)
G (E pos. III)
F (E pos. I)
in re-turn, hon-ey.
is to give me
my proper respect when you get

C (A pos. III)
F (E pos. I)
C7 (A7 pos. III)
F (E pos. I)
home. Yeah
ba-by, when you get
home.

C7
F (E pos. I)
C7
R - E - S - P - E - C - T
find out what it means to me,
R - E - S - P - E - C - T

F (E pos. I)
C7
F (E pos. I)
take out T - C - P.
a lit-tle re -
spect.

ARETHA FRANKLIN

Barre Chord Positions:

C♯ = E pos IX; F♯ = E pos II; D = E pos X;
A♭ = E pos IV; E♭ = E pos XI; B♭ = E pos VI.

G♯m = Em pos IV; B♭m = Em pos VI; Cm = Em pos VIII;
Dm = Em pos X; Bm = Em pos VII.

Bm = Am pos II; C♯ = A pos IV; Dm = Am pos V;
E♭ = A pos VI; F♯m = Am pos IX.

rhythm patterns on the bass strings

An effective way of setting up a strong rhythm and blues beat is to play a moving bass pattern, used by all R & B guitarists. We'll try this first in the Key of E:

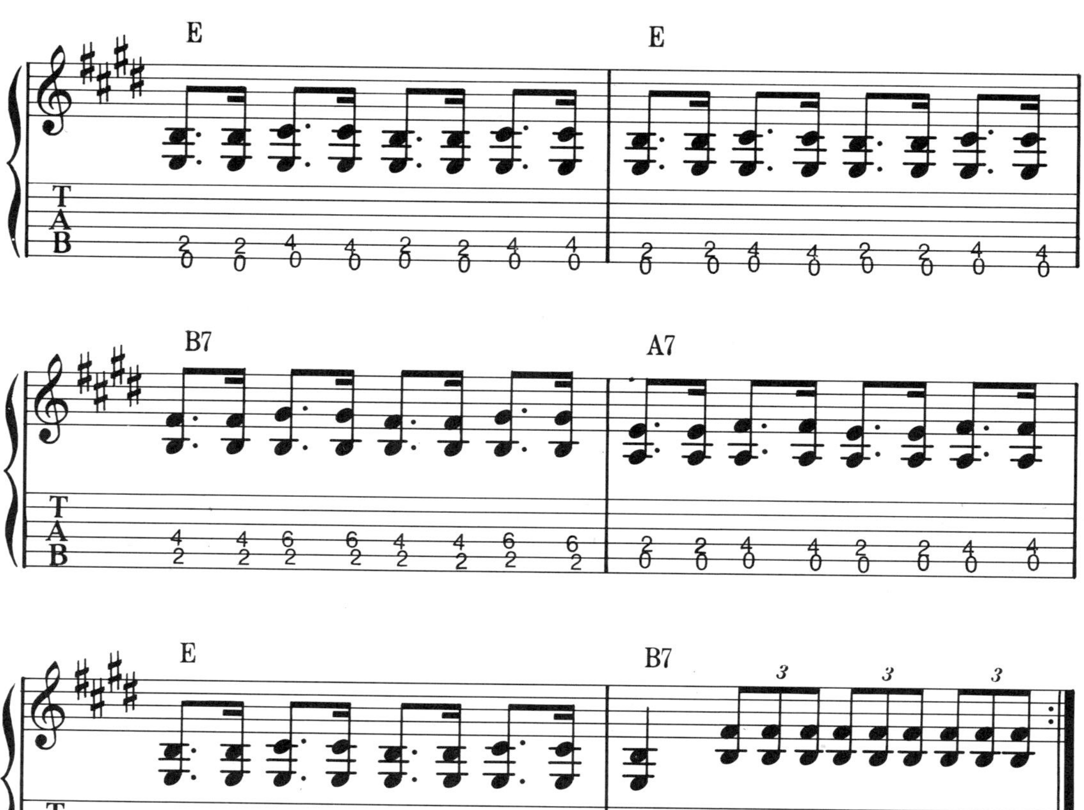

In order to play this pattern in the key of A, you would move the entire position up one string, so that now you are starting on the 4th and 5th strings. Here it is in A, with a slightly different rhythm:

In the key of G, you would use the E position barred on the third fret, playing the bass pattern as you did in E:

When you change to the C chord, you keep the barre where it is, but move your bass pattern to the 4th and 5th strings:

To play the D pattern, simply move that C up two frets:

In this way, any chord in any key can be broken down to this bass rhythm pattern. Try it in the keys of C, A♭ & F.

When playing this pattern, it is important to use sharp, downward strokes with the pick, hitting only the two strings that are to be heard. Damping the strings right after they are picked, and "muffling" the strings slightly with the heel of your right hand, can make the sound crisp and the rhythm stronger.

In listening to rhythm and blues performances, these rhythm patterns will be heard again and again, especially by such blues men as Jimmy Reed, Howlin' Wolf, Chuck Berry, and Muddy Waters. Just about any traditional blues will fit this beat. Here again is *See See Rider,* one of the most well-known:

See See Rider

E7
see what you done,
done,
T
A
B
A
A7
See See Rid - er,
see what you done,
E
done,
You
B7
A7
made me love you,
now your man done

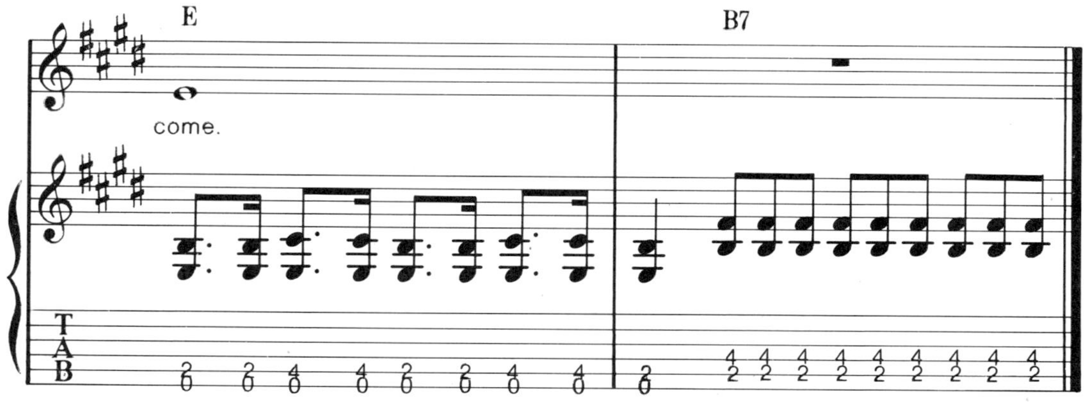

MISSISSIPPI JOHN HURT

That R & B bass line can also be played with a harmony line, which gives it a fuller sound. In the key of E it looks like this:

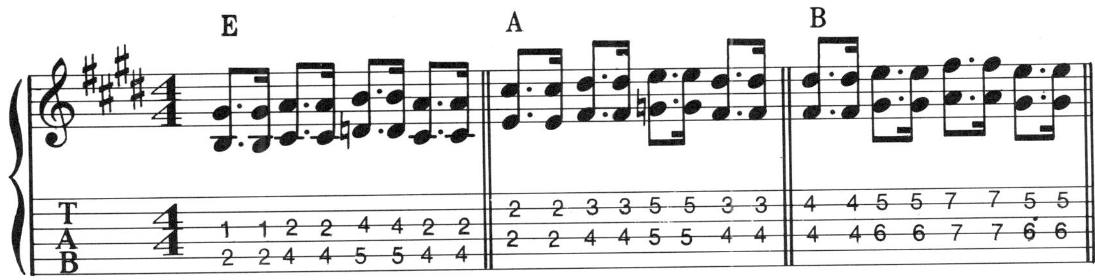

You will notice that since you are fretting the third and fifth strings in the E section of this progression, but *not* the fourth string, it is necessary to damp that string so that it doesn't sound. The finger that is fretting the fifth string can easily touch the fourth, thereby stopping the vibrations. Your pick stroke will have to be fairly accurate to avoid hitting the other open strings. The same, of course, is true in the A and B sections as well.

As in other chords where there are no open strings, these can be transposed easily by moving the whole progression up or down the neck. For instance:

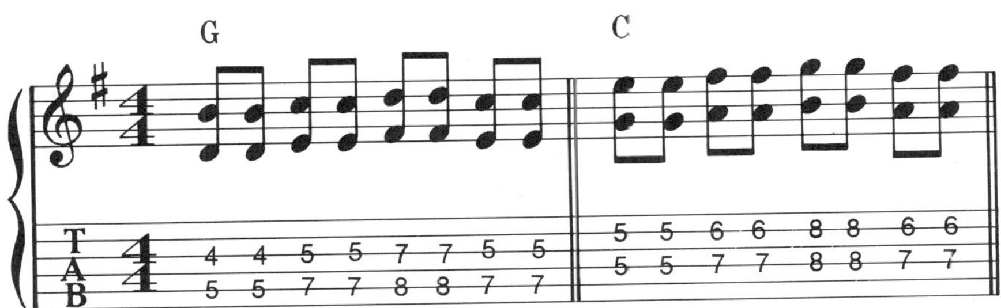

new chords

The following chords can be extremely useful if they are used correctly as substitutions for other chords. As they involve only three strings you must be careful to damp the other strings around them:

Learn the following E7 positions:

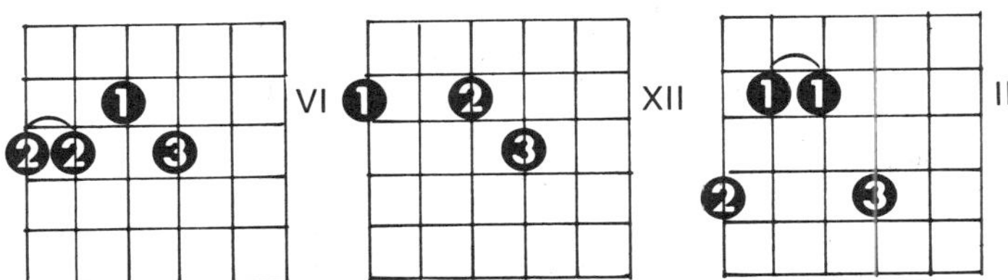

Learn the following A7 positions:

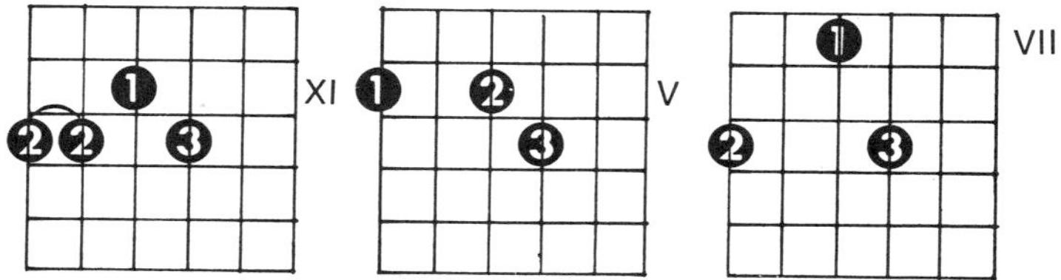

These B7 positions:

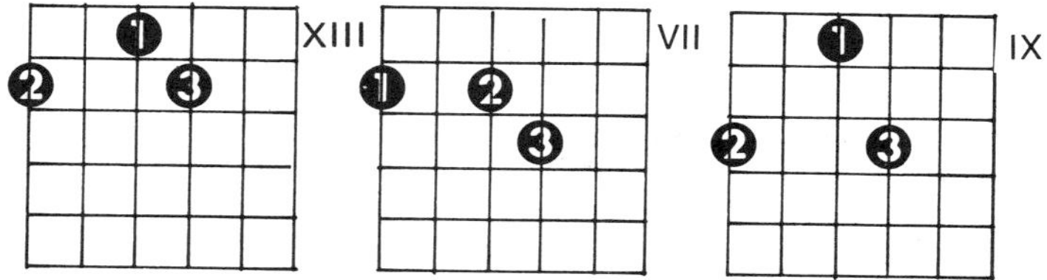

Apply these chords to *The Things That I Used To Do* a hit recorded by James Brown and Chuck Berry.

These chords can be transposed into different keys by moving them up or down the fingerboard. In fact, their great value lies in their movability, as well as in their jazz-oriented sound.

Minor chords can also be played in these three-note positions:

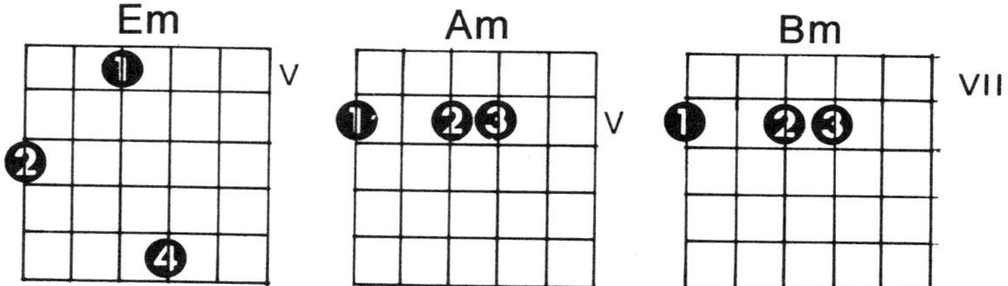

Try this exercise to practice these positions:

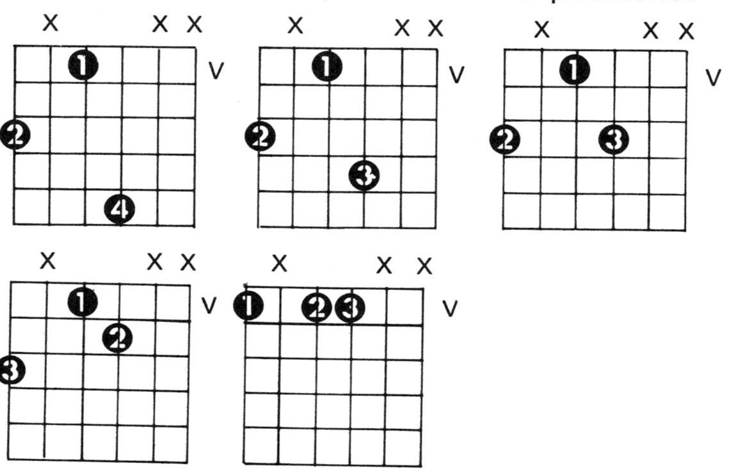

Now we will put the minor and major chords together so that you will actually be playing a blues "turnaround" with them:

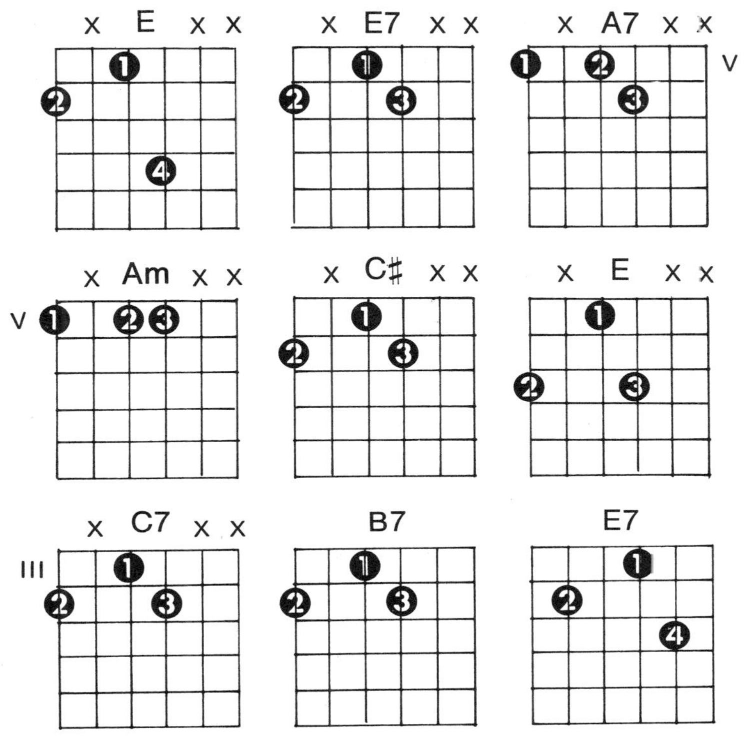

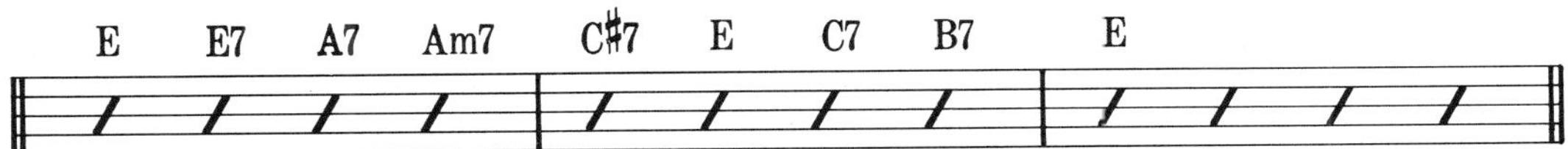

The following slow blues has been recorded by Chuck Berry, Guitar Slim, and James Brown. Try using the rhythm chords you have just learned to give the song new excitement. The last two measures of the song, the turnaround, are written above.

The Things That I Used To Do

By Eddie "Guitar Slim" Jones

the country sound

The "country sound" has become increasingly popular in Rock n' Roll, as reflected in songs such as *Act Naturally, Daydream, I've Just Seen a Face, Memphis,* and many of Bob Dylan's songs. The basic rhythm strum has been used in country and folk music since the '20s and '30s by such singers as The Carter Family, Jimmy Rodgers, and Woody Guthrie, and has been carried on in the Country and Western music groups. Of course, "country" guitar picking can get very complex, and the recordings of Merle Travis, Chet Atkins, and Doc Watson are highly recommended.

Here is an all-purpose rhythm strum in the "country" style:

The pick hits a single bass string on the first beat. (It will take some practice before it is clear and precise as it should be.) On the next beat, the pick brushes down across the top three or four strings, and brushes back across the same strings on its way to the next bass note. The rhythm should sound like *bum*-did-dy, *bum*-did-dy.

DOC WATSON

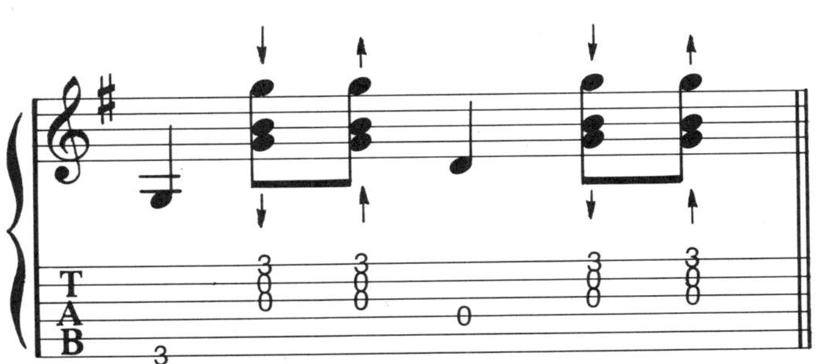

A slightly more complex version of this strum goes like this:

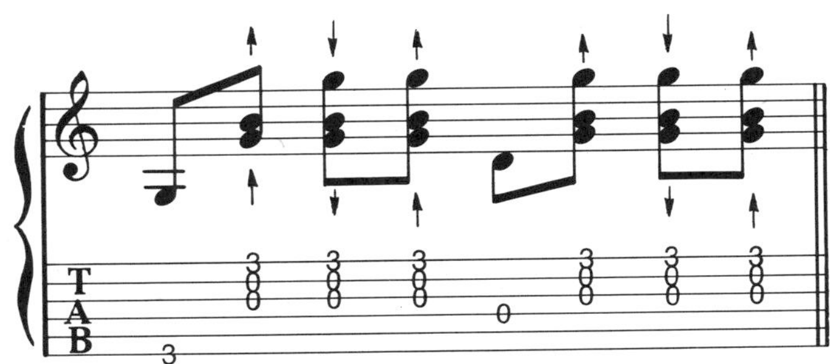

MERLE TRAVIS

Try this type of strum with one of Bob Dylan's earliest songs, Talking Folklore Center.

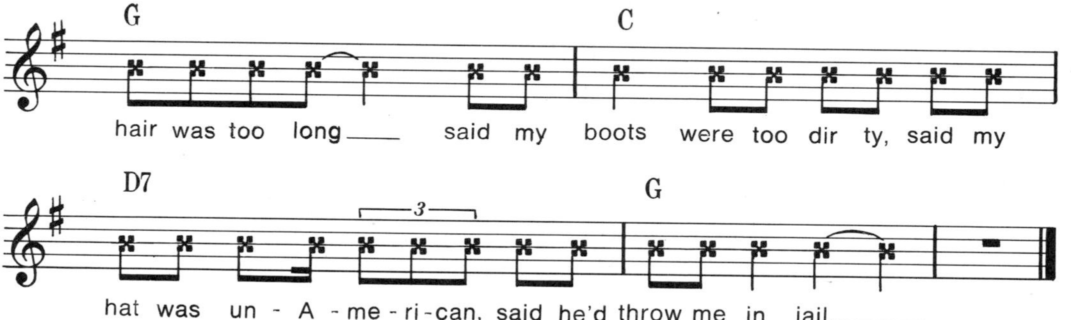

2. So I got on a subway and took a seat
Got out on forty-second street
I met this fellow named Delores there
He started rubbin' his hands thru my hair
I figured somethin' was wrong so I ran through 10 hot dogs stands,
4 movie houses and a couple a dancing studios to get back on the subway train.

3. The wind it blew me north and south
It blew me in a coffee house
I met this fellow with sun glasses on
He told me he sung folksongs
I believed him 'cause he was wearing sun glasses.

4. He sung "Scarlet Ribbons" 'bout ten times or more
He sung "Michael row the boat ashore"
He sung "Where do all the flowers go?"
There was no folksong he didn't know
The ones he didn't know he didn't like anyway.

5. On MacDougal Street I saw a cubby hole
I went in to get out of the cold
Found out after I entered
The place was called the Folklore Center
Owned by Izzy Yong -he's always in back- of the center.

6. They got real records and real books
Anybody can walk in and look
You don't have to own a Cadillac car
Or a nine hundred and fifty dollar guitar
Do like most people do -walk in -walk around- walk out.

7. But that's not the way you see
That ain't the way it oughta be
There's just one way a lookin' at it
You shouldn't take this place for granted
That'll always be here.

8. So go down and buy a record or book
Don't just walk around and look
You can do that when you go uptown
When you come down here you're on common ground
Common people ground -common guitar people ground
WE NEED EVERY INCH OF IT!

chops

Very often, the rhythm guitarist will play a very simple, sparse rhythmic figure throughout a song. He plays chords, sometimes in the low positions, and sometimes high on the neck, on the top three or four strings, adding a sharp, percussive beat to the song. Here are some of the rhythms that can be played:

A sharp sound can be achieved by damping the strings with your left hand immediately after striking them with the pick.

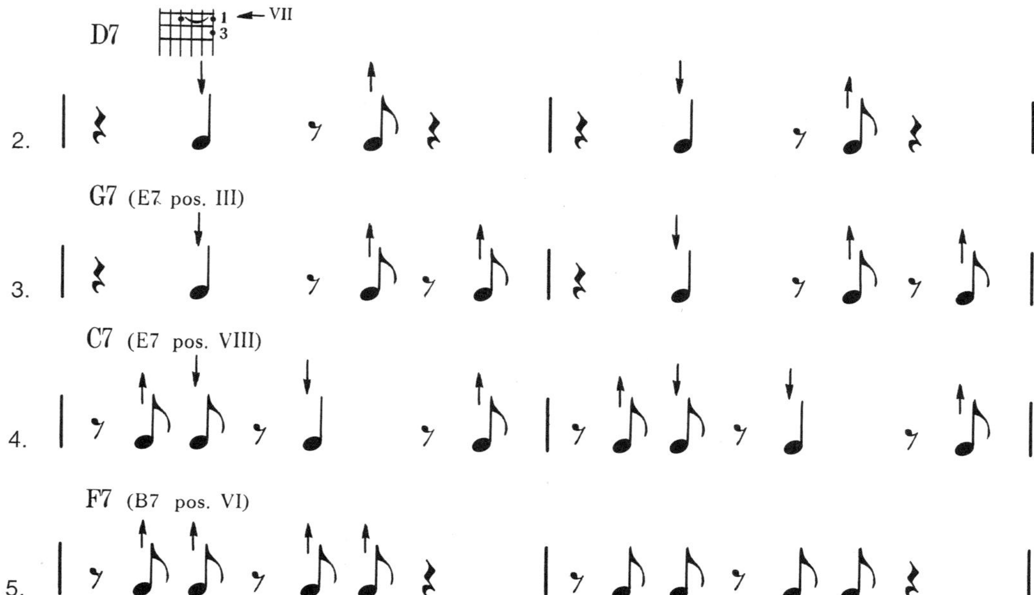

This effect can be heard on many records; listen to: *She's a Woman* (Beatles), *Taxman* (Beatles), *Hitchhike* (Stones), *Down Home Girl* (Stones).

miscellaneous rhythms

Here are some other blues rhythm patterns that are found in many songs, and that can be extremely useful to any rhythm guitarist.

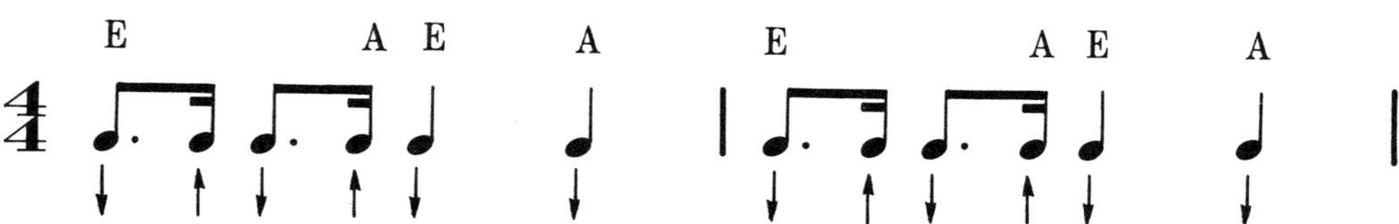

E A E A E A E A
A (E pos. V) D (A pos. V) A D A D A D
E A E A E A E A
B (E pos. VII) E (A pos. VII) B E A (E pos. V) D (A pos. V) A D
E A E A E7
A (E pos. V) A (E pos. V) G (E pos. III) A (E pos. V)
E7 (C7 pos. V)
TAB
7 7 6 7 7 6 7 7 6 7 7 6
7 7 6 7 7 6 7 7 6 7 10 11

House Of The Rising Sun

Now that you are familiar with various techniques of rhythm guitar, you can go on to work with several well-known songs.

This first song, House of the Rising Sun had been transformed many times before it became a number one hit by The Animals in 1965. Originally a traditional blues, Leadbelly arranged his own version, as did Bob Dylan, from whom The Animals apparently got their inspiration. The rhythm part is in triplets with an accent on the one of each measure:

(E7)
Am (Em pos. V)
C (E pos. VIII)
D (E pos. X)
There is a house in New Or -
F (E pos. I)
Am (Em pos. V)
G (E pos. III)
C (A pos. III)
leans, they call the Ris - ing Sun,
E7 (C7 pos. V)
Am (Em pos. V)
C (E pos. VIII)
D (E pos. X)
It's been the ruin of man-y a poor
F (E pos. I)
Am (Em pos. V)
E7 (C7 pos. V)
Am (Em pos. V)
E7 (B7 pos. VI)
girl, and me, oh God I'm one.
T
A
B

You Need Me

This next song, by Eric Kaz of Bear, *is called You Need Me. The rhythm is in the brisk, happy-time feeling made popular by The Lovin' Spoonful.*

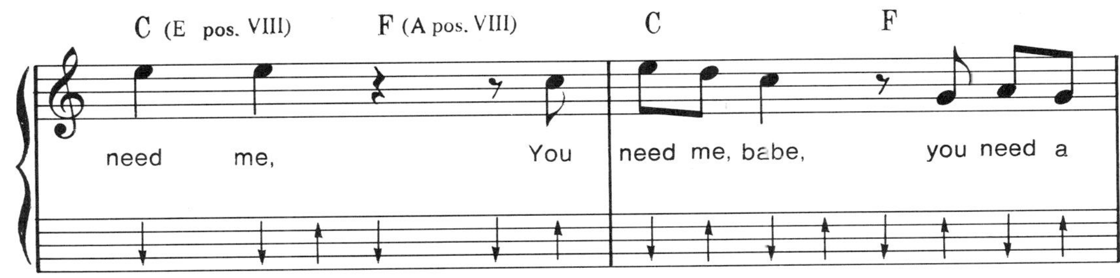
C (E pos. VIII)
F (A pos. VIII)
C
F
need me, You
need me, babe, you need a

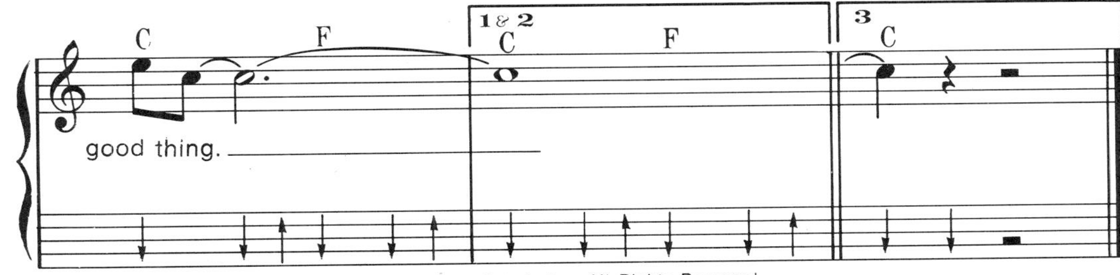
C
F
1 & 2
C
F
3
C
good thing.

ERIC KAZ

Slippin' and a-slidin'

This song, Slippin and Slidin is indicative of the many up-tempo rock-blues which use bass string figures for the rhythm part. Slippin and Slidin has been recorded by Little Richard, The Everly Brothers, Buddy Holly, and many others.

2. Oh, big conniver
Nuthin' but a jiver
Ah done got hip to your jive.
Oh, big conniver
Nuthin' but a jiver
Ah done got hip to your jive.
Slippin' and a-slidin'
Peepin' and a-hidin'
Won't be your fool no more.

3. Oh, Malinda
She's a solid sender
You know you'd better surrend.
Oh, Malinda
She's a solid sender
You know you'd better surrend.
Slippin' and a-slidin'
Peepin' and a-hidin'
Won't be your fool no more.

Midnight Hour

The final rhythm guitar example is the Midnight Hour. The guitar accent here is on the second and fourth beats, just as it was in Respect.

OTIS REDDING

Lead Guitar

There can be no beginning or end to an instruction session in lead guitar. The possibilities are as endless as the number of people who play the guitar. After all, a person's music reflects a part of his personality. I have seen the quietest of individuals banging savagely on a set of drums, and the most boisterous playing subtle lyrical themes on the guitar.

I remember all too well visiting a "rock" club in Edinburgh, Scotland. After descending three subcellars below the surface I found myself in a large, smokey, cavern-like cafe. The band, a group of Scots country boys, were imitating — note for note, nuance for nuance — a well-known Chuck Berry arrangement. They were doing a fairly good job of it, but after the third such imitation, I could feel how divorced these kids were from their music. I kept waiting for them to add an original note, an original idea, but it never happened.

At about the same time, the Beatles had released their song *Rain,* which uses various drone sounds commonly heard in Scottish music. The contrast was striking. The success of the Beatles is at least partially attributed to their continual experimentation with folk, country, blues, baroque, and Eastern musical sounds. They draw upon the sounds they hear around them, and mix them with their natural feeling for the music of their *own* country, to come up with their original and natural sound.

It is important to listen to the music of other cultures and to experiment with it in your own songs. Of course, it often becomes the "in" fad to sound as far out as possible. There are many groups around the country who are experimenting with sitars, tamboras, kotos, etc. and many of these experiments work. Unfortunately, though, they often deteriorate into a self-conscious hodge-podge of unpleasant sounds. The most important thing is to listen carefully to the music of other countries, try to understand that music, and let it influence your playing by drawing from it what you need to develop ideas.

Artie Traum

JOHN LENNON AND PAUL McCARTNEY

using the pick for lead guitar

Since most rock guitarists use a flat-pick (plectrum), it is essential that you learn to use the pick, and develop the speed and accuracy that you will need to play lead guitar. The following exercises should help you to build your right hand technique. Start each exercise slowly, gradually accellerating your speed until you can play it easily, producing clean, sharp, tones.

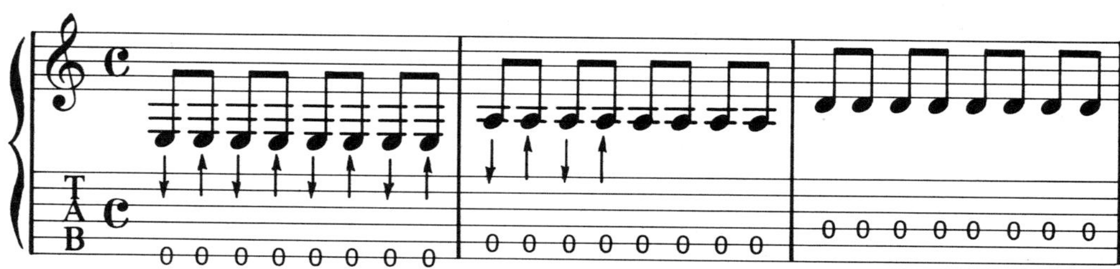

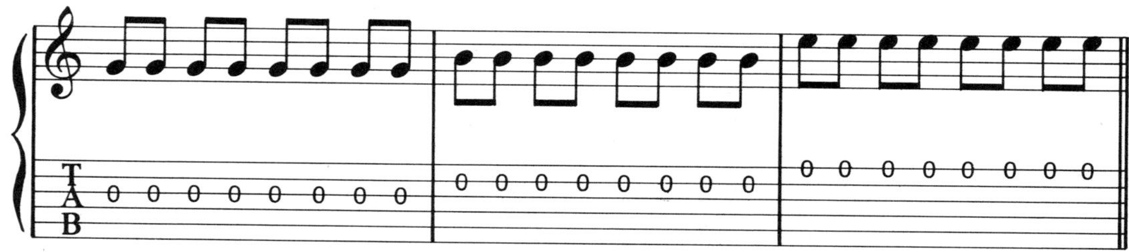

In playing arpeggios, or broken chords, you will have to play different strings with the pick direction changing on each string. This exercise has practical value in that similar runs are used when the lead guitarist fills in with arpeggios behind a singer, usually singing a quiet ballad. Try this general technique to accompany *Mr. Tambourine Man* (Dylan); *It's Only Love* (Beatles); *As Tears Go By* (Stones); *Turn, Turn, Turn* (Byrds); and *Lucy In The Sky with Diamonds* (Beatles), as well as many other songs of this type.

This exercise makes use of three and four-string movable chords. Any chord can be moved from its basic position to a position up the neck, as long as you are not picking any open strings. As with the barre chords, each fret raises the chord sound by one half-step. If you finger a D chord and move it one fret higher, you have a D♯ or E♭ chord (provided you pick only the top three strings, of course). The D position on the fourth fret would give you an E chord (two frets above the original D position), at the seventh fret you would have a G chord.

Similarly, the small F position can be moved up the neck to make a G (third fret), A (fifth fret), C (eighth fret).

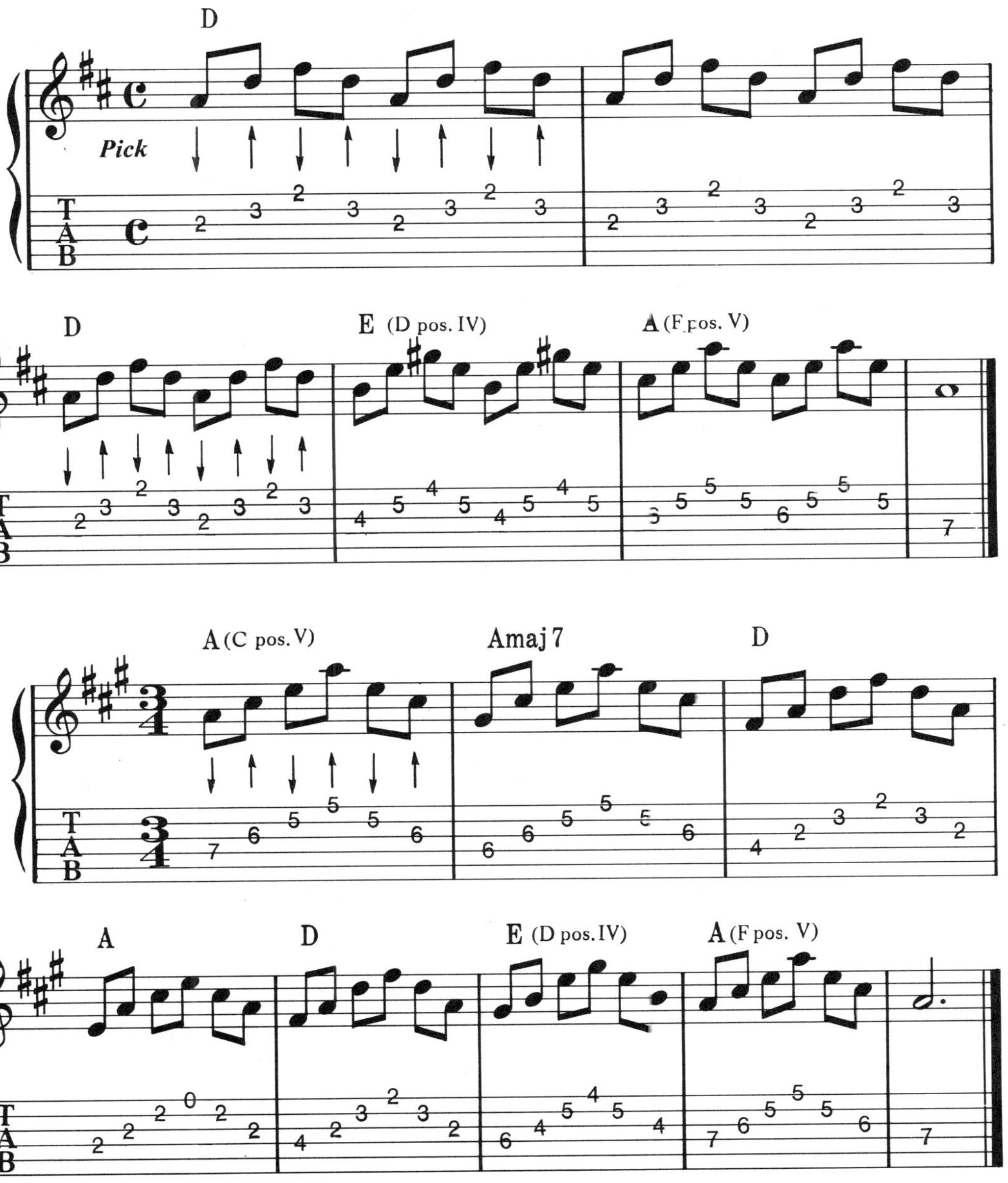

D
Pick
D
E (D pos. IV)
A (F pos. V)
A (C pos. V)
Amaj 7
D
A
D
E (D pos. IV)
A (F pos. V)

The pick-strokes are often done in other patterns, for greater speed and efficiency, as in this exercise:

F (D pos. V)
G (D pos. VII)
C (F pos. VIII)

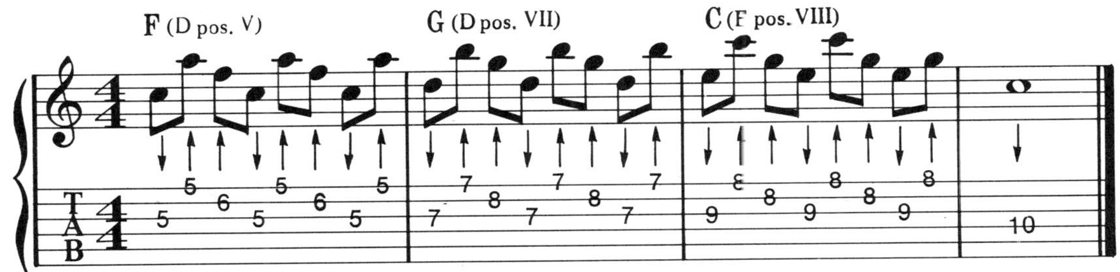

finger stretches

It is always a drag to practice exercises on the guitar, or, for that matter, on any instrument. But if you try the following exercises for just a few moments every day I think your technique will improve considerably.

We will start with a rather difficult exercise designed to stretch your fingers a little. First, make the following position on the tenth fret:

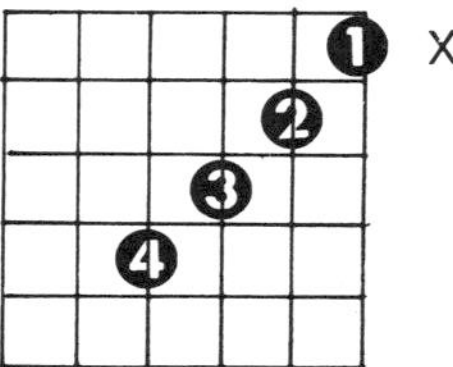

then move your first finger one fret:

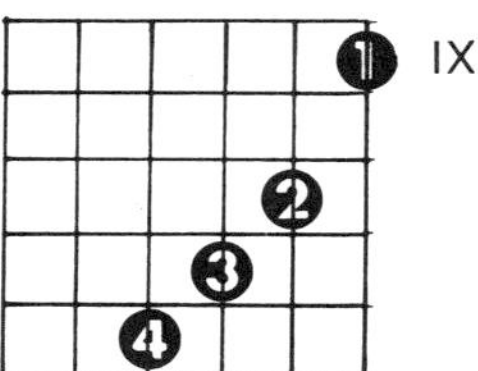

then your next finger:

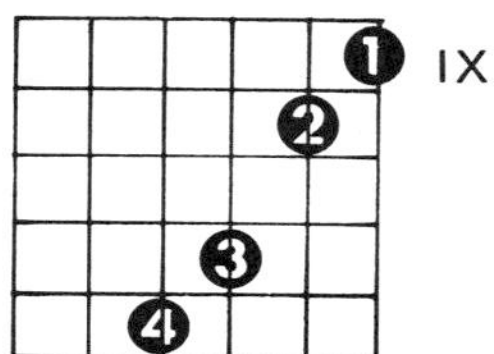

then your third:

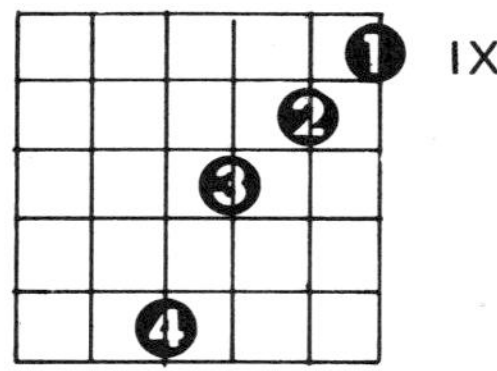

then your pinky.

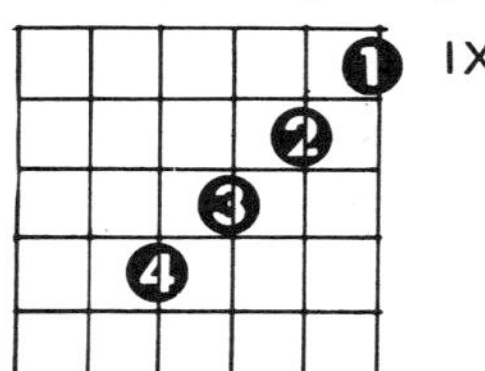

You should have reached your original position one fret lower. Continue doing this until you are on the first fret. Then work your way back up the neck. If you can do this easily then you are doing something wrong. It may even take a bit of practice to get the initial position. You'll find your fingers getting sore . . .

Here is a good solo-speed exercise. The first finger of your left hand will play the first string, first fret; the second finger will play the second fret; third finger plays the third fret; and fourth finger plays the fourth fret. Now play each of the following combinations of fingering, starting slowly and *evenly,* building up speed and accuracy gradually on each one. The pick should be alternating between down and up strokes.

1-2-3-4	4-3-2-1	2-1-3-4	3-4-1-2
1-4-3-2	4-2-3-1	2-3-4-1	3-1-4-2
1-3-2-4	4-1-3-2	2-4-3-1	3-2-4-1
1-4-2-3	4-3-1-2	2-4-1-3	3-1-2-4

Once you start getting these on the first string, move on to the others. Remember to take it slow and easy, gradually building up speed.

blues runs

Since a major part of our popular music derives from the blues, much of the improvised breaks and lead solos are based upon blues scales. The notes of these scales can usually be improvised into a lead solo, and the more familiar you get with these scales the more interesting and musical your breaks will be. We are showing these scales in the key of A, but they are movable, and can be transposed to any other key, simply by moving them up or down the neck of the guitar. Therefore, if you want to play a run in C, move it up three frets, using the same fingering positions as you did for A.

The first blues scale is based around this A chord:

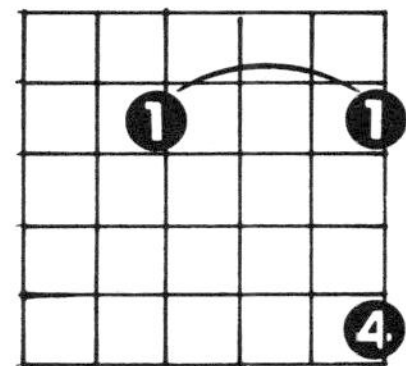

The same run can be played in a different position.

The next is based (loosely) around this A chord position:

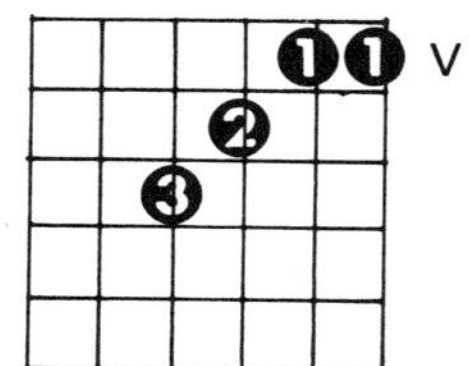

Here is a run that is very useful, and can be played in different positions:

Practice these runs over and over until you are familiar with them, not only in the key of A, but also in G, C and E♭.

The next step is to break up these scales into a lead guitar solo, using the 12-bar blues form. These solos can be played in an infinite number of ways, and no two guitarists would play them exactly alike.

We have added the rhythm guitar part because we feel that the best way to practice is to jam with someone else. Get a friend to play the rhythm while you play the lead, and then switch, so you both get the practice of playing both parts. (If you can't find a friend who plays, get a hold of a tape recorder and tape about a dozen choruses of the rhythm. Then play it back, adding the lead part to your rhythm.)

Rock Solo 1

A
E7
D7
A
E7

MIKE BLOOMFIELD

Here is another blues-rock solo in A, this time set to an 8-bar blues pattern, and using slightly different runs. A typical rock-guitar sound can be achieved by adding harmony notes to the run. The rhythm guitar plays the same back-up as in the last example.

Rock Blues
Solo
2

RHYTHM
A
LEAD

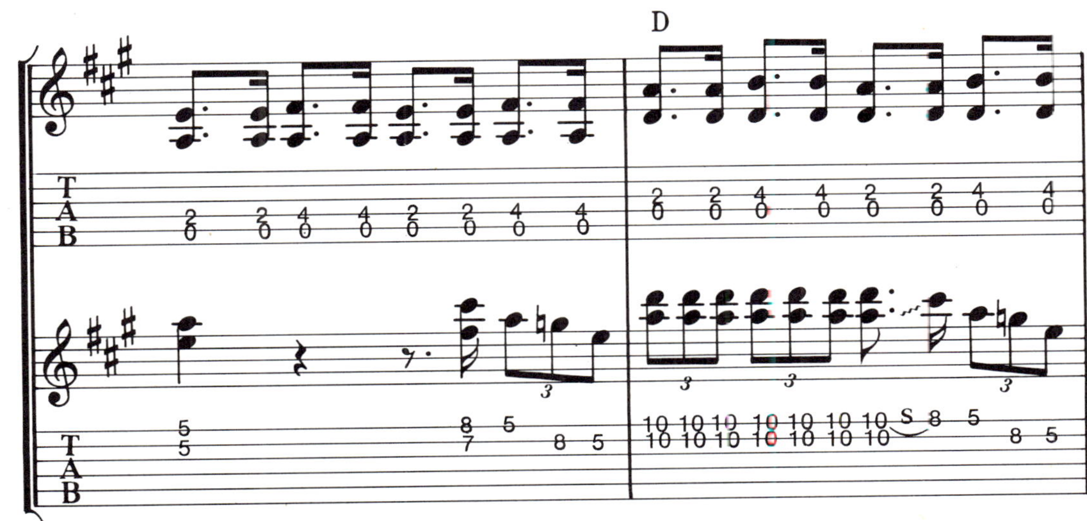
D

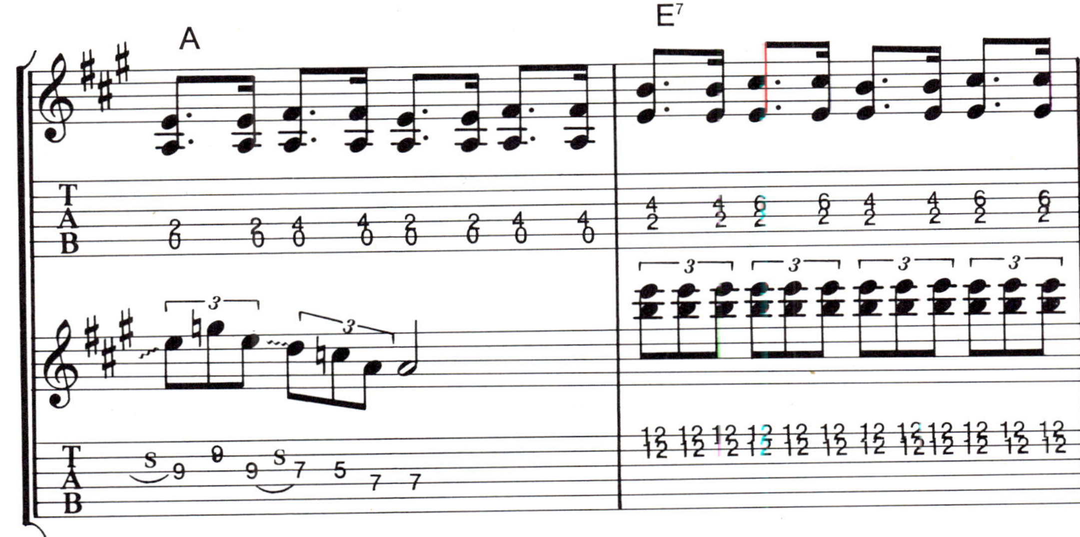
A
E7

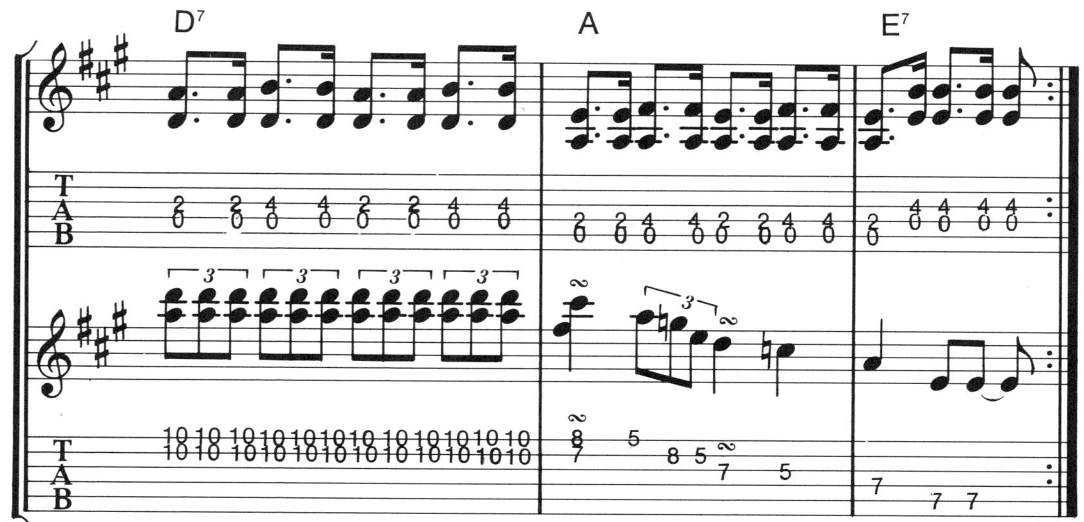

Here's a solo in a medium-fast tempo done in the style of the great Elmo James, one of the best of the blues singers, who recorded his finest tunes in the early 1950's.

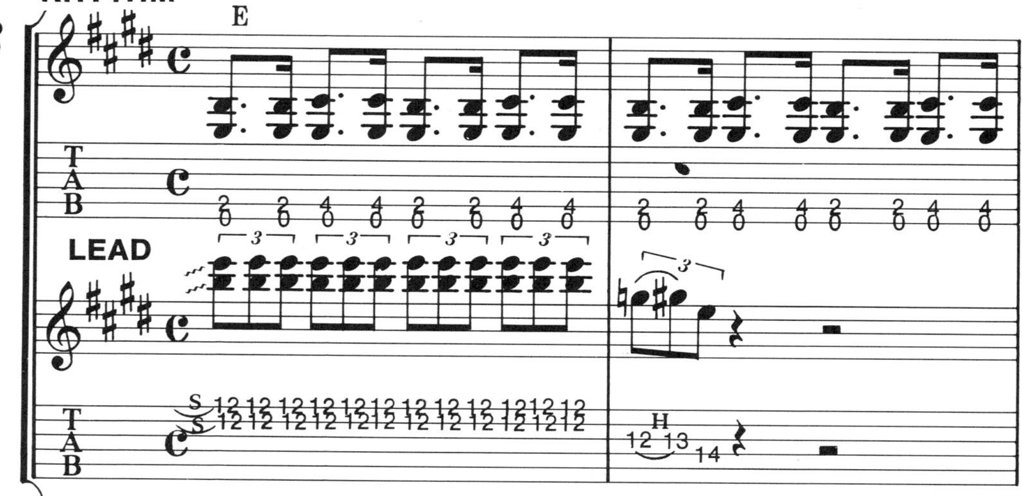

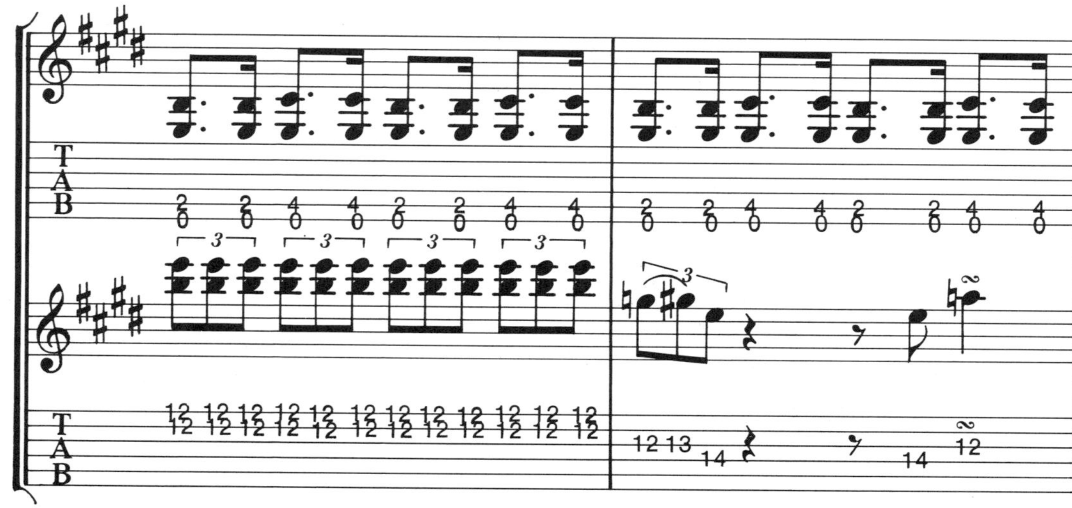

ALBERT KING

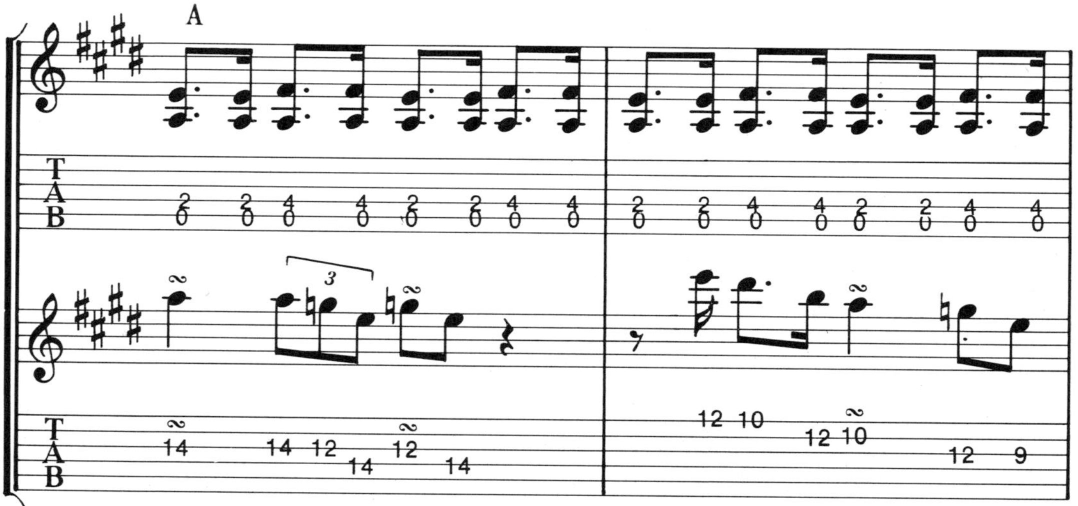
A
T
A
B
T
A
B

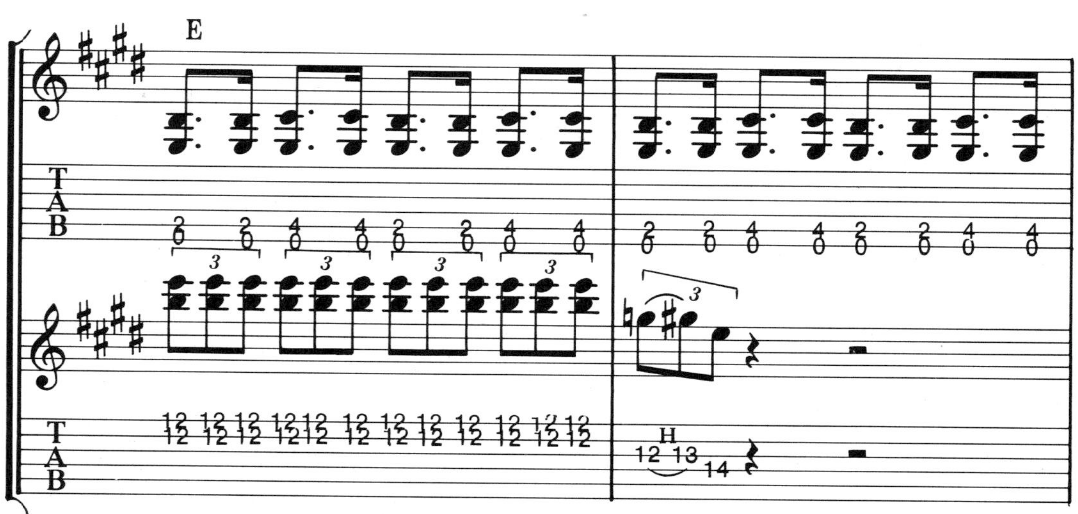
E
T
A
B
T
A
B

B7
A7
T
A
B
T
A
B

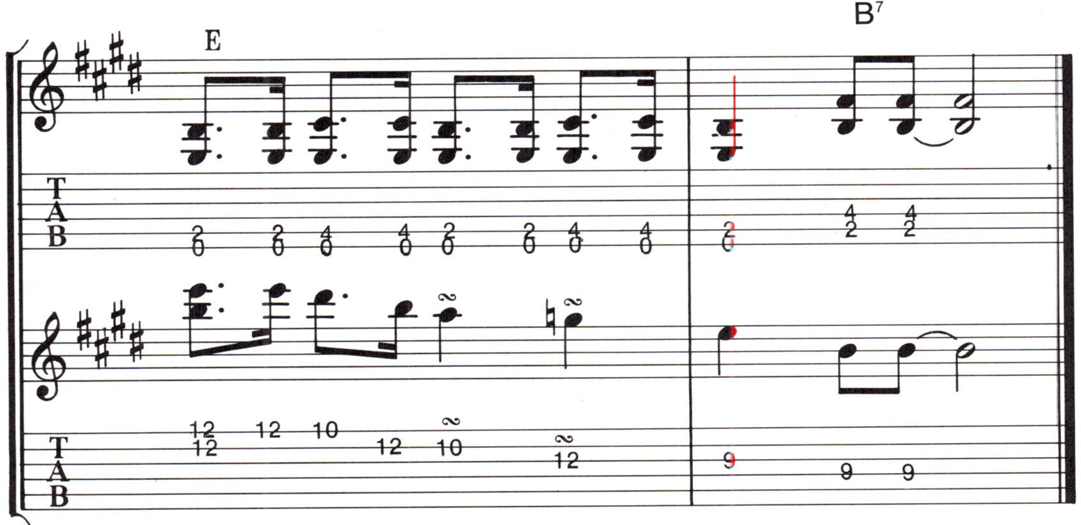

bass lines for guitar

Every good song has its own distinctive bass or treble figure which is usually played by the lead guitarist. We have included below some well known bass figures to give you an idea of how to approach this problem:

T
A
B
5 7 7 5 7
0 2 0 2
0 2 2 0 2
2
B♭
3
4
4
8 8 6 6 6 H 8 6
6 6
E♭
B♭
F
10 10 8 8 8 H 10 8
8 8

B♭
3
E
A
E
B
E

4
G7 (E7 pos.III)
C7 (E7 pos.VIII)
G7 (E7 pos.III)
D7 (E7 pos.X)
C7 (E7 pos. VIII)
G (E7pos. III)
D7 (C7pos.III)

SAM ANDREW, LEAD GUITARIST FOR JANIS JOPLIN

Remember that Rhythm and Blues bass line on page 41 A line almost identical to that one, done in the treble, can be played as a lead accompaniment to a blues tune, or even as a lead break. This is the way it would look in the key of A. Try transposing it to other keys by sliding this pattern up or down the fingerboard to the appropriate frets.

NOTE: The D and E sections may also be played:

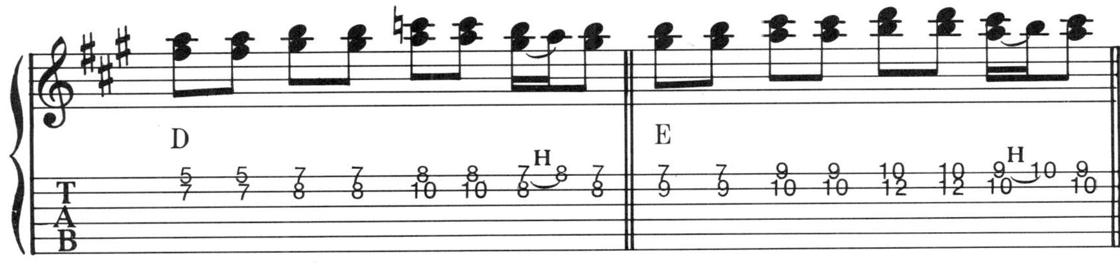

Hi Heel Sneakers

2. Put on your hi heel sneakers
wear your wig hat on your head. (2x)
We'll play that show now baby,
'cause I know you gonna knock 'em dead. Heh!

THE CREAM

Short Fat Fanny

Following is a transcription of the introduction to Little Richard's Short Fat Fanny as he recorded it for VJ Records (#1107).

A7
Don't wan-na rip it up, don't wan-na work with An-nie, I
E7
got a brand new love her name is Short Fat Fan-ny. One
day when I was vis-it-ing Heart-break Ho-tel, That's
where I met Fan-ny and she sure looked swell. I
A7
told her that I loved her and I'd nev-er leave her, She
E7
put her arms a-round me and she gave me fev-er. She's
A7
my tut-ti frut-ti and I love her so,
E7
Watch-ing like a hound-dog ev'-ry where I go. When
A7
ev-er I'm a-round I'm say-ing P's and Q's,

B7
She might step on my blue suede shoes. While at a
E7
honk - y tonk par - ty just the oth - er night,
Fan - ny got jeal - ous and she start - ed a fight be -
A7
cause I was danc - ing with Mar - y Lcu, I had to
E7
call Jim Dan - dy to the res - cue.

This is a possible lead guitar break for The House of the Rising Sun. See section I for the rhythm part.

ERIC BURDON
AND
DANNY KALB

Rock Me Mama

The following traditional blues *Rock Me Mama* was recorded by Judy Roderick on Vanguard Records. The guitar solo was transcribed from that recording.

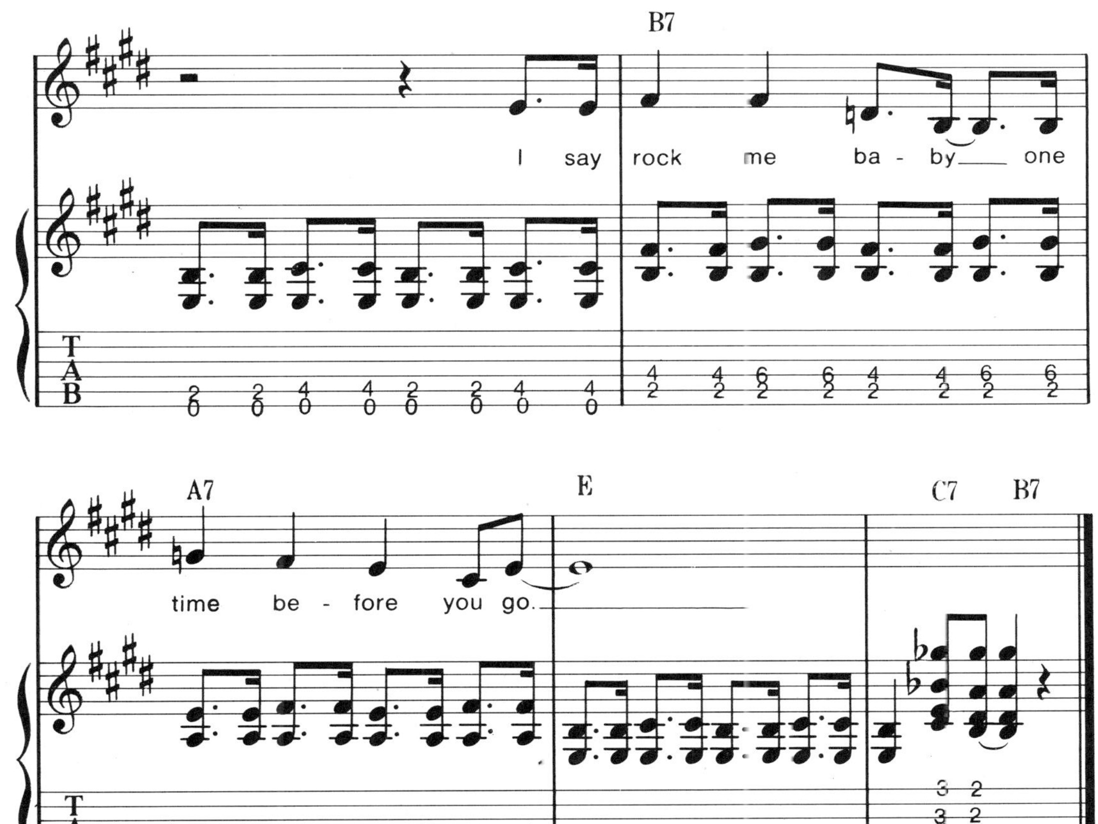
B7
I say rock me ba - by one
A7
E
C7
B7
time be - fore you go.

Lead Guitar Solo
A7
E
T A B

B.B.King

This section is the most difficult, and therefore the most valuable in the book. It contains five transcriptions of solos taken by B. B. King. Each solo is a distinctive unit; it is important that you listen to the recordings of these pieces before attempting to play them.

We have included portions of an interview with B. B. King as they appeared in Jazz Magazine in February, 1967.

B.B. King an interview by Stanley Dance

I was born on a plantation right out from Indianola, not too far from Itta Bena. Most of my boyhood was spent around there. My father and mother separated when I was about 4, and my mother carried me up in the hills of Mississippi. She passed away when I was about 9, and I spent a lot of time alone then, because my father didn't know where I was.

I worked for the white people my mother had worked for. I lived by myself, but they fed me and let me go to school. The school was a one-room building, with one teacher and about eighty-six kids, and that was where I got most of my elementary education. I had to walk five miles each way — ten miles a day. I didn't think much about it then, but now I wonder how I did it. I used to milk ten cows in the morning and ten cows at night. These people I worked for didn't have much money, but I got about fifteen dollars a month. Now, believe me, it was one of the happiest parts of my life, because there, then, they were just simple people. Today, I find, people are different. You've got to be at a certain level to be recognized, but then, whoever you were, you were that particular person.

My uncle there was married to a lady whose brother was a sanctified preacher. The preacher used to play guitar in the church and afterwards he would usually go back to my uncle's to visit his sister and I would always go along too, because I liked to fool with his guitar. I liked it so much that I later asked my boss if he would get a guitar for me that a friend of his had, and take it out of my wages. He did that, and I never forget that red guitar with a round hole in it. It cost eight dollars.

That was how my musical career began, but there were no teachers of music through there that I ever heard about. Four of us boys got a little quartet together, but I wasn't interested in blues then. I always thought I might be able to get somewhere in the spiritual field. The Golden Gate Quartet were our idols, and we'd hear them on the radio. I learned by just watching and listening to that preacher play. I kept fooling with the guitar and I learned three chords. It seemed as though I could sing almost anything with those three chords, like 1, 4 and 5.

Then I began to run into different guys who were playing guitar, and I'd ask them things. I met Robert Junior Lockwood and Sonny Boy Williamson, and it was Sonny Boy who later gave me my first break. The work scene was fairly plentiful. They'd play the plantation halls and joints where a lot of gambling went on. The men who ran them would hire any name that would bring the people in. Those that danced went into the dance-hall part, and those that wanted to gamble went in the other. A guy who could draw could easily get a guarantee of two or three hundred dollars, because the man who had the joint could probably make that much at the door, plus his gambling. Sometimes they'd have a trio, and sometimes it might be Sonny Boy alone — and you'd be surprised how they'd dance to just him and his harmonica.

It was a funny thing, but it was when I went in the army that I started singing blues. A lot of fellows seemed to get religious and sing spirituals when they got in there, but me, I didn't. When I got home I realized a lot of fellows were making a living singing the blues, but my people were very religious and I was afraid to sing the blues around the house. My aunt — I did the spiritual album for her a few years ago — would get angry with anyone singing the blues. I would have to do that away from the house, but I found later on that people seemed to like me singing and playing.

So I would work all the week and sometimes on a Saturday I would have eight or ten dollars. I would take this money and buy me a ticket to the nearest little town — me and the guitar. I would go to this little town and stand on the corners and play. The people seemed to like it and they would tip me a nickel, a dime or a quarter. That sort of thing is still done in the South. Sometimes on a Saturday I'd visit three or four towns, sometimes as far away as forty miles from where I lived, and sometimes I'd come home with maybe twenty-five or thirty dollars. So I found I made more in that one day than I had in the whole week. The money was nice, but that wasn't all of it to me. I wanted to do it, and it made me feel good that they enjoyed listening to me.

Later on, the war was over, and I went to Memphis and got a job. It was about a hundred-and-thirty miles north, but to me that was like going to Europe. I had never been out of Mississippi except when I was in the army, but I had heard of Memphis and W. C. Handy, and I wanted to see what it looked like. Two of us hitch-hiked from Indianola to Memphis, and I found my cousin, Bukka White, who was living there.

They had just opened the first radio station — WDIA — with Negro personnel in Memphis. (It was white owned.) I went over there and walked into the station with my little guitar on my back. I saw a man called Nat Williams — he was a professor, but he was working as a disc jockey then — and he asked what he could do for me. "I want to make a record," I said. I don't know what made me say that, because I didn't go there to make a record, but to get on the air. He called Mr. Ferguson, the general manager. He asked me my name and I told him, Riley B. King.

"Do you play that thing you have on your back?"

"Yes."

So when I started playing and singing for him, he liked it, and it gave him an idea.

They'd just got a new product called Pepticon, which was going to be competition for Hadacol, a tonic that had been big. He called the program director and he said, "We've got ten minutes open, from 3:30 to 3:40, with nothing set. Let's put him in there." So I sang a couple of songs. They didn't pay me, but I could advertise where I was playing, and that was my objective in the first place. After that, they would bring me on every day as the Pepticon Boy, and later this got so big that they had to give me more time.

I got me a little trio with Johnny Ace on piano and Earl Forrest on drums, and on the two nights I had off from the lady's place I would go out and do one nighters. Even before I got the trio, I could earn twenty-five dollars by myself. I didn't know what to do with all this money, and I messed it up. I started drinking and gambling a little bit. Guys would give me stories, too, and I was very generous. I don't regret that.

When one of the disc jockeys left the station, they made a disc jockey out of me, and they said I'd have to get a new name. The product that sponsored me was selling so well, and I was on the air for them fifteen minutes a day for about fifty dollars a week. It got so popular that on the Saturday the salesmen would take me to the little towns outside Memphis, and we'd have a big truckload of the stuff, and I'd sit there singing, and they'd get rid of any amount of this tonic that was supposed to be good for tired blood. One of the salesmen said they would listen to me because they could see I had an honest face!

The first name they gave me on the station was *The Boy from Beale Street,* and then it got to be *The Beale Street Blues Boy.* The people got hip and started calling me "B. B.", and that was how the name B. B. King came about. I did very well and got very popular, so when another disc jockey left they gave me his show, too, and I ended up with two hours and fifteen minutes a day.

I really began to fight for the blues. I refused to go as Rock n' Roll as some people did. The things people used to say about those I thought of as the greats in the business, the blues singers, used to hurt me. They spoke of them as though they were all illiterate and dirty. The blues had made me a better living than any I had ever had, so this was when I really put my fight on. A few whites gave me the blah-blah about blues singers, but mostly it was Negro people, and that was why it hurt. To be honest, I believe they felt they were trying to lift the standards of the Negro, and that they just didn't want to be associated with the blues, because it was something still back *there.*

To me, it wasn't like that. If Nat Cole could sing in nightclubs and be a great, popular singer; If Frank Sinatra could sing his songs and be a great person; if Mahalia Jackson could sing spirituals and be great — why couldn't I be a blues singer and be great? Then there were so many young people who wanted to play like me, and sing like me, that I wanted to bring it up to a level where they could be proud.

The blues are almost sacred to some people, but others don't understand, and when I can't make them understand, it makes me feel bad, because they mean so much to me. It's something like a kid being whipped for something he didn't do. He has no defense and he just has to take it. That's how it is with me and the blues some . . .

I remember my childhood, how things were with us then, the race problems, and how bad it was in the '30s. I remember how it hit us. After that there was my life with modern people, and then there were the tragedies I experienced. I could never talk to anybody about it, so it all just stayed with me. It's like a guy making a joke about having the largest feet in the state: "Oh, boy, do I have large feet!" But he knows he does have large feet, and you can take it as a joke or vice versa. And so the blues became a part of me right on from Blind Lemon Jefferson and Leroy Carr. I heard them on records. I heard Lonnie Johnson, too, and I idolized him. My great aunt used to play them on her Victrola, and I would hear them every time my mother took me to see her.

I remember so many things that happened to me as a boy, and they have influenced the way I play and sing. There are a lot of novelty songs you can sing and be happy with, but when you dig down it's like going to church or something. You're getting to something that you believe in, that you believe is true. It is a little bit different when it has happened to you, or to someone you know. Then you feel very bad when someone criticizes it. Maybe some people don't want to be reminded that it happened to them, too.

Bukka White was another influence on me when I was a boy.

BUKKA WHITE

The older people know him, just as they know Big Maceo, Tampa Red and Leroy Carr. A lot of the singers who were based in Chicago toured the South, because that was where the best audience was. The blues-minded people were mostly those who were born and raised down there. They did more for the artist than the northern cities. These people brought their idea of how it should be, and usually their records, when they came north. Then, too, guys like Blind Lemon came to Chicago, but they would usually go back. Another guitar player I liked very much was Buddy Walton. I heard him in Memphis.

Bukka was a lot older than me, and he used to record. He had a steel bar he would put on his finger, and the sound he'd get from the strings with it would go all through me. I never could do that, but I learned to trill my hand, and with the help of the amplifier I could sustain a tone. Sounds are more important to me than trying to play a lot of notes. It's like automobiles. You can have speed or economy, not both. I practice scales, but then I go right back to trying to get certain sounds. About two years ago, I started taking up the clarinet, and I learned to read very well with it. Of course, I found that as long as I had wind to blow I could sustain a note, and I thought, "Why can't I sustain like this on the guitar?" I've been trying to do this for years, but the last two or three I've really gone into it. I think I've made a little progress. On the slow tunes I know, I try to play guitar as if someone was blowing a horn. I think the clarinet suggested this and helped.

I like to be original. I always like to have something new, and if other guys like it well enough to copy, then I try to get something else. I continue to study every chance I get, but I come back to the sound. I still haven't got the sound I actually want, but I think I'm pretty close to it.

I've got my favorites among musicians, of course. I went down to hear Kenny Burrell the other night, and he's a very fine guitar player. George Benson made me feel like throwing the guitar away. In the jazz field, two of my favorites were Django Reinhardt and Charlie Christian. And back with the blues, I like T-Bone Walker.

My ambition is to be one of the greatest blues singers there have ever been. I've had a lot of things in my favor. I'm trying my best to get people who don't like the blues not to hate them. You may not like something, but you can still respect it. Maybe I'm defending what I'm doing, but when I stand on the stage and sing and sing, and people don't understand what I'm doing, I almost cry. I've seen people of another blues field get on the stage, and the crowd give them such a rough time that I've felt sorry for them.

If people tell me I'm a good artist, I appreciate it. To say myself that I'm great, that I can do this, or that I can move the people — I've never had that kind of confidence. So therefore I'm a little bit timid. Sometimes, when I'm going out for a walk with a friend, he may meet someone he knows and says, "Say, man, this is B. B. King." I don't have the word to use for it, but it can make me feel real little, because maybe this guy he's introducing me to has never heard of B. B. King. I remember one time a guy introduced me to some girls, because he wanted to stop and chaff with them. I was just beginning to get popular then. "Hey!" he said, all excited, "I want you to meet B. B. King." One of the girls asked, "Who is B. B. King?" I could have gone through the floor, and that has stayed with me all these years. I really shiver when anyone introduces me in that way.

That's one of the reasons why I've tried not to change too much. When I go out on that stage, I'm scared half to death. My knees rattle after eighteen years. Same thing in a club, although I'm more comfortable there than in a theatre.

That brings me to my big question. Why is it blues singers aren't on TV? They sell a lot of records and they have a big audience, just like the Beatles, who sing their songs, or Mahalia Jackson who sings her spirituals. The TV people go from jazz to spirituals to pop, but they never give blues singers a break. I've watched programs like Ed Sullivan's for a long time, but they can't know what kind used one. They have folk singers on TV, but I'm a blues singer! Now what's the difference? I'm singing about things I've actually experienced.

The B. B. King pieces which follow are transcribed with the help of Larry Leitch.

Blind Love

2. Well, standing on the corner
 between 35th and Main (2x)
 Well, a blind man seen my woman
 and a dumb man called her name,

3. He said, "Oh I'm blind,
 you brought eyesight and made me see!" (2x)
 The dumb man asked the question,
 "Woman who can your good man be?"

4. Well, I'm standing here trembling, darling
 with my heart here in my hand (2x)
 Well, I can tell my baby's face
 Lord, I ain't got no man.

Lead Guitar Solo

1. No mat-ter what you say Babe, no mat-ter what you do, The

way you're been treat-in' me wom-an___ I's com-ing back home to you. And your

cry - ing won't help you wom - an, cry - ing won't help you

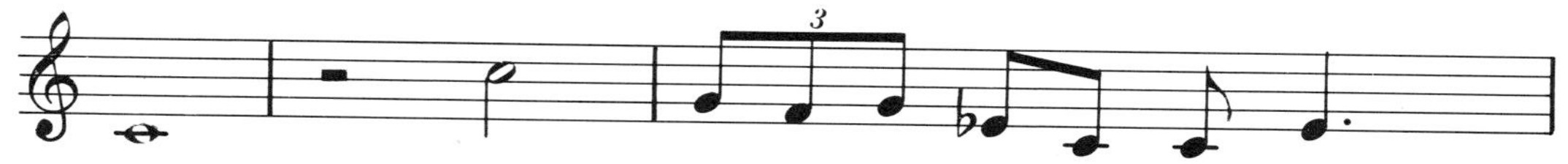

Babe. Yeah, cry - ing won't help you wom - an,

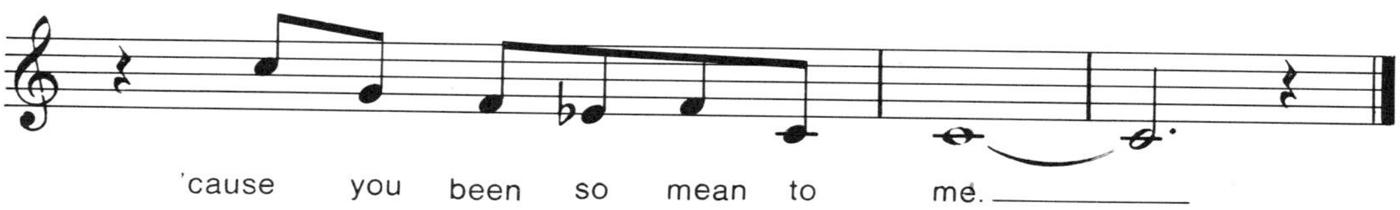

'cause you been so mean to me.________

2. You must remember, babe,
 no matter where you go,
Watch those seeds you scatter, woman,
 'cause you gonna reap just what you sow.

3. The way you treat me, woman,
 I just can't understand,
I'm gonna leave you, woman,
let you do the best you can.

And your (Chorus)

4. Just before I leave you, woman,
 just want to shake your hand,
I'm gonna get me a woman
 - let you get you a man,

And your (Chorus)

Lead Guitar Solo

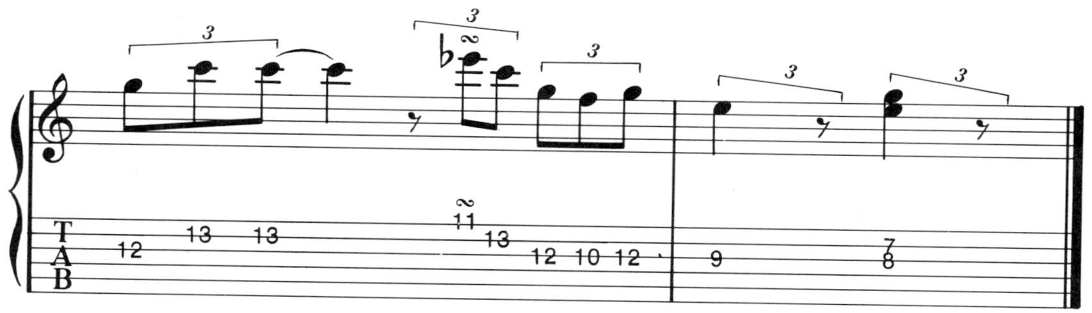

I Want To Get Married

2. Yes I've only been in love but three times in my life
The first said I could'nt satisfy her but I've
only been in love three times in my life
The second was a juice head and the third was
another man's wife.

3. Well, they say join the navy if your really
wanna see the world (2x)
Well, I say join B. B. King babe if you really
wanna be loved.

4. Well, my time has come babe
and I must say goodbye (2x)
You women better watch out, I've gotta have
that wife before I die.

Lead Guitar Solo

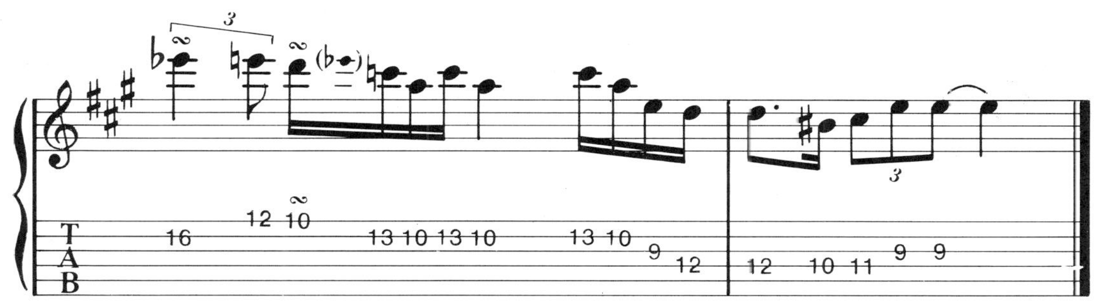

2. She's not too tall, complection is fair
Man, she knocks me out the way she
wears her hair.

3, I tried to describe her
it's hard to start
I'd better stop now because I got a
weak heart.

Lead Guitar Solo

Ten Long Years

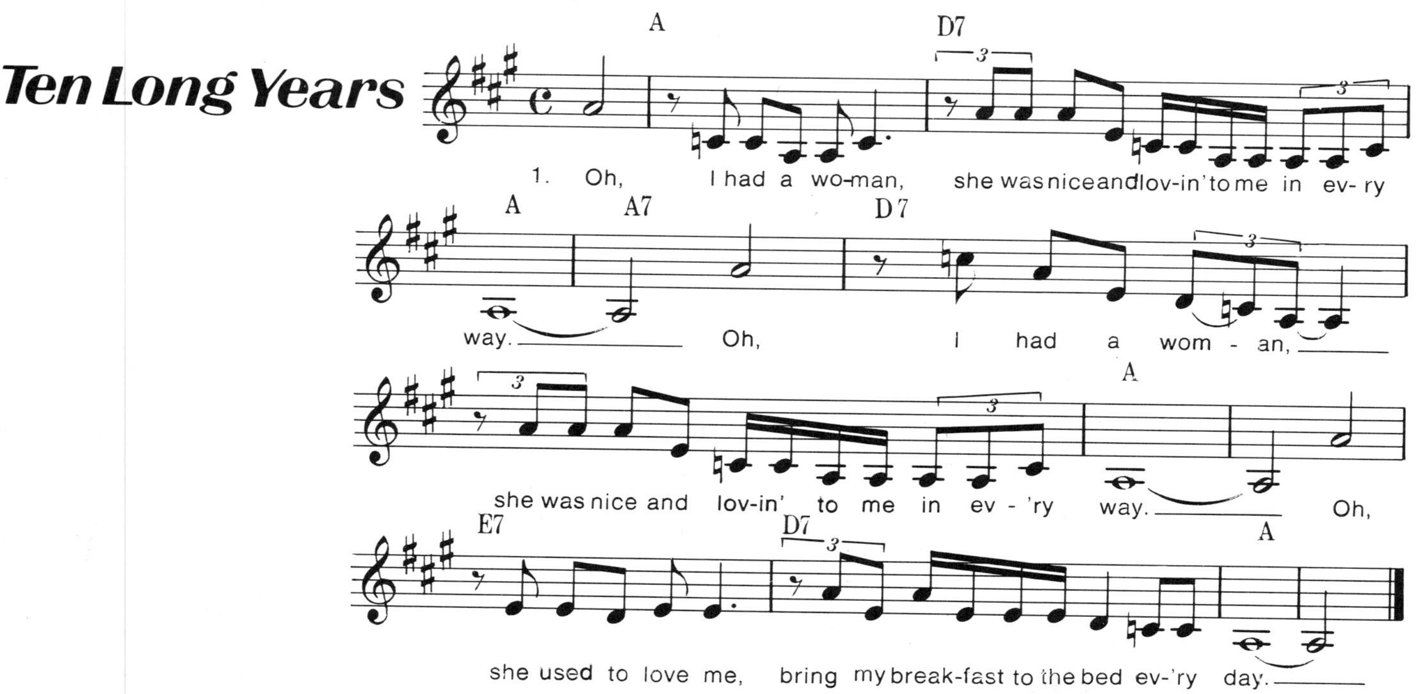

2. Oh, for ten long years,
   yes she was my pride and joy. (2x)
   Well, I used to call her my little girl
   And she used to call me her little boy.

3. Well, it's all over baby,
   babe you know I'm all alone. (2x)
   Well the reason I sing these blues
   Yes, you know my baby's gone.

Lead Guitar Solo

Appendix

Buying an electric guitar

With the current boom in guitars steadily growing, guitars are being sold in department stores, record shops, pawn shops, bargain basements, electrical supply outlets, and even in some music stores. There are guitars selling for $12.95 including amplifier (not recommended) and guitars that cost a thousand dollars without amp. If you are looking for a guitar, and are puzzled by the tremendous variety of names, styles, looks, colors, and sizes of guitars, perhaps we can help you with some general information about buying a new guitar.
WHERE TO BUY IT: If you live in a large city, there is probably a large music supply store that sells instruments at a discount, such as those stores on 48th street in New York City. These stores usually give between 20% and 40% discount on instruments and accessories. I would recommend that you deal with a reputable music store, rather than a pawn shop, bargain store, etc. This is especially true if you are new to guitars, since a guarantee on any instrument is very important. It is possible for a person who knows a lot about guitars to get a good buy in a used instrument by dealing with pawn shops or the classified sections of local newspapers. A teacher or friend might be able to help you out in this way.

Like any instrument, electric guitars are cheap or expensive according to the materials used, the workmanship, etc. Most beginning students will not want to spend much on their first instrument, but I feel it is important to learn on a fairly good guitar. A cheap guitar will give you more trouble than it's worth. The sound will be bad, it may warp, the action will probably be high, making the instrument hard to play. Of course these things may not be true, but it has been my experience that a name brand with a guarantee will save you a lot of headaches in the long run.

A fairly decent solid-body guitar will start at about $100.00 and go to about $250., depending on the make, the number and quality of the pick-ups and the general craftsmanship. A hollow-body electric would cost more, starting at about $175.00

What to look for when buying a guitar

In buying any fretted instrument, the most important thing to look for is a good neck — that is, one which is perfectly straight, with an easy action (this is usually adjustable, depending on the type of bridge), and one in which the frets are perfectly in place so that the strings are in tune at each position on the neck. If you do not know how to check these things out, here are a few hints.

To be sure the neck is straight, sight down the length of it from the nut, then turn it around and do the same from the place where the neck joins the body. You can easily see any dip or bulge in the fingerboard this way. If you have a good musical ear, test the frets by sounding the open string, then fretting it at the twelfth fret and sounding it again. The tone at the twelfth fret should be exactly an octave higher than the open string. (If the octave is a little sharp or flat, check to see if the guitar has a movable bridge. If so, the trouble might be corrected by a slight adjustment in the placement of the bridge.) Now try the same thing at other intervals on the neck; the fifth fret (an interval of a fifth above the open string), the seventh fret (a sixth), etc. Test the frets on each string as well as at different intervals.

Even if you are getting an inexpensive guitar, you will probably want two pick-ups to get the sound you want; one for the treble frequencies for playing lead, and the other for the deeper bass tones, for playing rhythm.

The decision as to whether to get a solid-body or hollow-body guitar is primarily a matter or taste.

The trend, as of this writing, is towards the solid-body. Although these guitars don't have that high-pitched, screaming quality associated for so long with rock guitar, they are more versatile in variations of tone. The hollow-body guitars are able to produce a wide spectrum of sounds, from a natural "guitar" sound used a lot in jazz, to the powerful electric rock sounds. In my opinion, though, there is nothing like a solid-body for that wild lead guitar treble.

There are dozens of makes of electric guitars on the market today, the most well-known being Fender, Gibson, Epiphone (a subsidiary of Gibson), Guild, and Gretch. These companies all make a variety of styles and models, from reasonably-priced to very expensive. Other names you might come across, especially in the lower-priced bracket are: Hagstrom, Framus, Rickenbacker, Vox and Standel.

It should be noted here that if you have a fairly good acoustic guitar, it can easily be converted to an electric by means of a pick-up microphone which is placed either under the strings in the sound-hole, or attached inside the guitar under the bridge. A guitar amplified in this way is made much louder, and the tone sustains much longer, but the quality is more like a loud acoustic guitar than an electric. Many people prefer this more natural sound, and it is especially good for country style or folk-rock guitar playing. A pick-up of this type will cost from $20 to $50.

Accessories

Many of the dynamic and unusual sounds that the rock groups are getting these days are made with gadgets such as reverberation and tremelo units, fuzz tones, treble boosters, volume-control foot pedals, etc. These accessories are certainly not necessary to produce exciting sounds, but if used tastefully they can do a great deal to expand the scope of your music. Of course, each of these things costs money, and most groups get them one at a time, depending on their need of the moment.

Buying an Amplifier

Like the guitar, amps come in all shapes, sizes, and prices. Once again, if possible, wait until you have enough money to get a good amp, rather than wasting your money on one that will distort the sound, short-circuit, blow fuses, etc. Unless you expect to be playing in large halls right away, it won't be necessary to get a really large amp. A small practice amp of fairly good quality would start at about $70, or $100.00 if you want reverb (a nice addition, but not absolutely necessary for a student). If you are playing in a group, you will probably want a better amp, and will have to spend about $150.00. Of course, you can spend as much as $1000 or more, but I wouldn't recommend it unless you have some pretty big jobs ahead of you.

The price of an amp usually depends on the size and quality of its speakers, whether it is equipped with reverb, tremelo, auxiliary inputs for other instruments, separate channels with tone and volume controls, etc.

A good group amp should have a minimum of 50 watt power, and have at least one ten or twelve inch speaker, in order to produce a good, undistorted sound. Some of the best-known and respected names to look for in amplifiers are: Ampeg, Fender, Gibson, Guild, Standel, Magnatone, and Vox.

Discography

A proper record collection should include examples of "country blues" guitar. The best are:

Robert Johnson   Columbia
Really the Country Blues   Origin
Country Blues Encore   Origin
John Hurt   Vanguard
Skip James   Vanguard

The best "city blues" recordings are:

The Best of Muddy Waters   Chess
The Best of Howlin' Wolf   Chess
The Blues (Volumes I and II)   Chess
Chuck Berry's Greatest Hits   Chess
B. B. King Live at the Regal   ABC Paramount
Albert King (*Born Under a Bad Sign*)   Stax

For "soul" guitar, especially rhythm parts:

Aretha Franklin   Atlantic
Solid Gold Soul   Atlantic
Jr. Walker's Shotgun   MoTown/Soul

The "new rock" sound is epitomized by Jimi Hendrix, Eric Clapton, Mike Bloomfield, George Harrison, etc. . . Listen to:

The Cream   Atco
The Blues Breakers   Atco
Auto Salvage   RCA Victor
Paul Butterfield Blues Band   Elektra

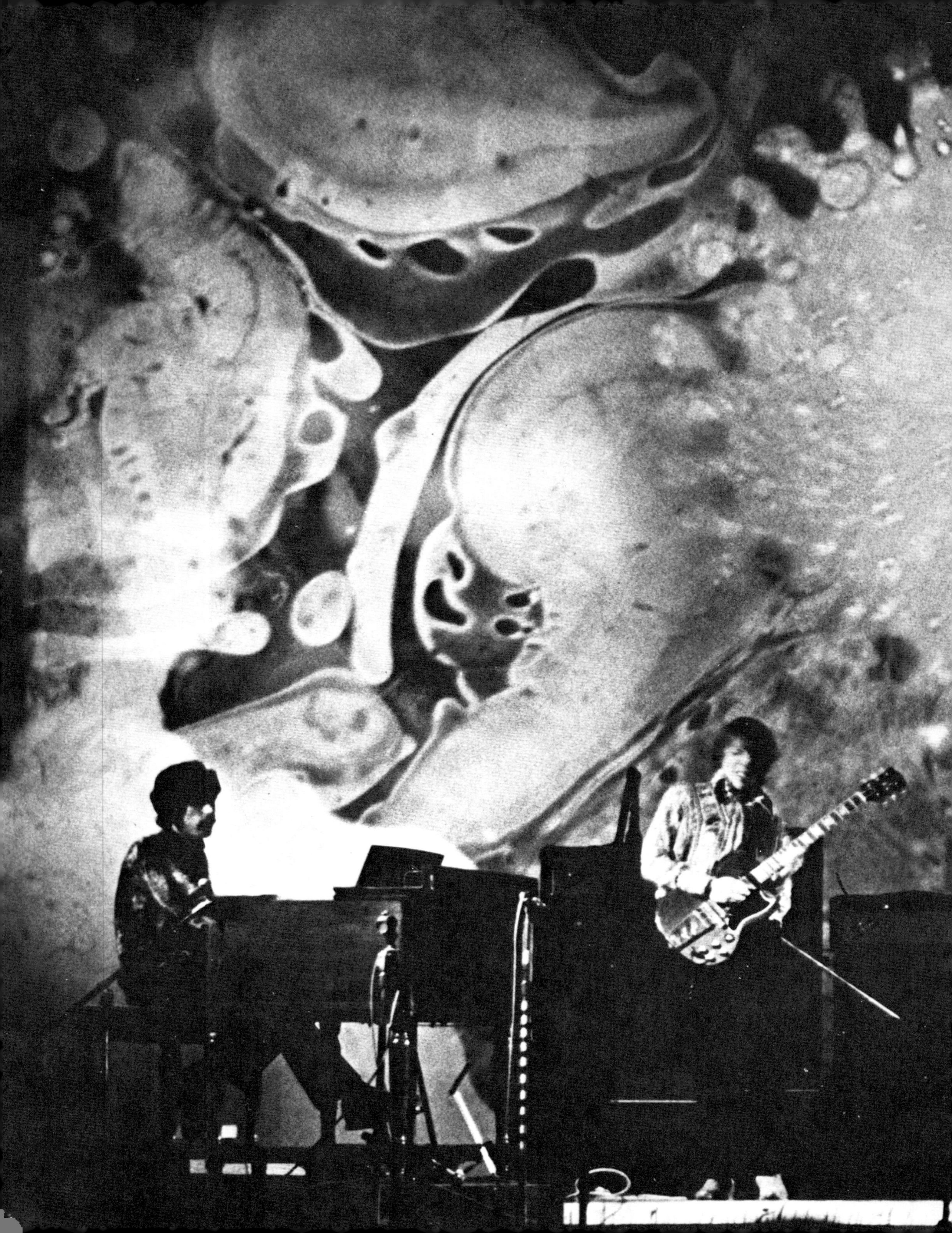